Building a Game with Unity and Blender

Learn how to build a complete 3D game using the industry-leading Unity game development engine and Blender, the graphics software that gives life to your ideas

Lee Zhi Eng

BIRMINGHAM - MUMBAI

Building a Game with Unity and Blender

First published: November 2015

Production reference: 1251115

Published by Packt Publishing Ltd.
Livery Place
35 Livery Street
Birmingham B3 2PB, UK.

ISBN 978-1-78528-214-0

www.packtpub.com

Credits

Author
Lee Zhi Eng

Reviewers
Matt Schoen
Tony V. Le
Gareth Wright

Acquisition Editor
Shaon Basu

Content Development Editor
Sumeet Sawant

Technical Editor
Edwin Moses

Copy Editors
Dipti Mankame
Jonathan Todd

Project Coordinator
Shweta H Birwatkar

Proofreader
Safis Editing

Indexer
Hemangini Bari

Graphics
Abhinash Sahu

Production Coordinator
Shantanu N. Zagade

Cover Work
Shantanu N. Zagade

About the Author

Lee Zhi Eng is a 3D artist-turned-programmer who is currently the cofounder-cum-chief technical executive at Reonyx Tech, a technology firm based in Malaysia.

Before he cofounded the company, he worked as an artist and programmer in several game studios before becoming a part-time lecturer for 2 years at a university to teach game development subjects related to Unity Engine and Unreal Engine. He has not only took part in various projects related to games, interactive apps, and virtual reality, but also participated in multiple projects that are more oriented toward software and system development, such as vehicle tracking systems, corporate management systems, web applications, and so on and so forth.

When he is not writing code, he enjoys traveling, photography, and exploring new technologies. You can find more information about him at www.zhieng.com.

About the Reviewers

Matt Schoen is an indie games developer and Unity guru. His primary focus is on systems and tools development with C#, but as a generalist, he's touched practically every feature of Unity. In his day-to-day work, he also uses Visual Studio, Maya, Blender, the Adobe Creative Suite, and a wide variety of creative and development software. He's worked with Unity since its early days and has been a part of the developer community for just as long. From presenting at and attending Boston Unity Group meetings and Unite conferences to participation in the Unify Wiki and Unity Forums, he has given and taken lots of help on a wide range of projects. He cofounded Defective Studios and has been proud to work on a wide range of internal projects and external contract work, including Archean Worldbuilder, CosmoKnots, and a number of collaborations. He is currently in the early stages of authorship on another PACKT title: Google Cardboard Projects with his co-author Jonathan Linowes.

Tony V. Le is an independent game and web developer who was born and raised in Chicago, IL where he attended Columbia College Chicago and graduated in spring 2015 with a Bachelor's Degree in Game Design and a Minor in web developer. Currently now attending graduate school at DePaul University for his Master's Degree in Computer Game Development, he had also started up his own company, tvledesign LLC, and is now working towards developing a professional career in both the game and web industry. With the ongoing passion to continue learning and developing new techniques, he not only takes on the role of being a student but he also loves to take on the role of being a mentor, teaching and inspiring others like himself to create and live for the passion they strive for.

Gareth Wright (known online by many as just Gruffy) has been an independent game developer since his graduation from the University of Plymouth with a bachelor of science honors degree in 2013. Using Unity 3D and the community-developed Blender, he has provided 3D art for the past three years to a number of clients and the community and for use in his own developments.

Due to *enjoyment of the problem*, as opposed to locking down one particular field, Gareth enjoys working in both desktop application and frontend web application development, but his main passion lies firmly with game development and using Unity3D or UE4 engine to give his modular environment developments life.

As a photographer, Gareth has provided reference photography for game companies seeking related reference shots due to his location near to the moors in Devon and also provides postprocessing imagery to keep his digital art skills fresh.

You can find him lecturing on software and game development at South Devon College, Paignton, to both FE and HE or at home in the office experimenting with some mechanic idea inspired by a game he recently played or online at Unity Answers looking for a challenging question or two.

Here's the list of his games:

- Tricade: This is a 3-player arcade game by *Andrew Cuffe, Adrian De Lurendium, Gareth Wright*.
- Houndtor: This belongs to Histories and Legends, and developed by *Gareth Wright*.
- Free Modular Environments: Unity Asset Store (Search "Gruffy") Blender pipeline
- Flingy: 2016 release by *Gareth Wright*

Other companies which I worked for:

- Particles of Sound by *Daryl Fensom*, Audio Engineer and scripting advisor
- Protectus Security Services Ltd: OpenCV image matching algorithm development (NDA)
- The Learning Clinic: Web application developer (NDA)

I would like to thank my family for the continued support at every turn in my life. My sister for her continued bravery, my brother for his continued devotion to progression, my mum and dad because they are simply the most amazing people anyone could ever hope to know.

Finally, thanks to technology and the technologists, without your knowledge and will to share it, I wouldn't be half as capable as I am today — just saying J.

www.PacktPub.com

Support files, eBooks, discount offers, and more

For support files and downloads related to your book, please visit www.PacktPub.com.

Did you know that Packt offers eBook versions of every book published, with PDF and ePub files available? You can upgrade to the eBook version at www.PacktPub.com and as a print book customer, you are entitled to a discount on the eBook copy. Get in touch with us at service@packtpub.com for more details.

At www.PacktPub.com, you can also read a collection of free technical articles, sign up for a range of free newsletters and receive exclusive discounts and offers on Packt books and eBooks.

https://www2.packtpub.com/books/subscription/packtlib

Do you need instant solutions to your IT questions? PacktLib is Packt's online digital book library. Here, you can search, access, and read Packt's entire library of books.

Why subscribe?

- Fully searchable across every book published by Packt
- Copy and paste, print, and bookmark content
- On demand and accessible via a web browser

Free access for Packt account holders

If you have an account with Packt at www.PacktPub.com, you can use this to access PacktLib today and view 9 entirely free books. Simply use your login credentials for immediate access.

Table of Contents

Preface

In the wake of the indie game development scene, game development tools are no longer luxury items costing up to millions of dollars but are now affordable by smaller teams or even individual developers. Among these cutting-edge applications, Blender and Unity stand out from the crowd as a powerful combination that allows small to no budget indie developers or hobbyists alike to develop games that they have always dreamt of creating.

What this book covers

Chapter 1, Creating Your Game Concept, will teach you how to design your own game, such as writing the game's story, choosing a visual style, and designing characters and environment concepts.

Chapter 2, Creating Characters, will be a step-by-step tutorial on how to create your game character in 3D using Blender.

Chapter 3, Animating Your Characters, will help you learn how to bring your game characters to life by creating different animations for the characters in Blender.

Chapter 4, Creating the Environment, will help you learn how to construct an astonishing 3D environment for your game in Blender.

Chapter 5, Integrating Your Assets into the Game, is a step-by-step tutorial on how to import your 3D assets from Blender to Unity and set up prefabs for later use.

Chapter 6, Developing the Game Structure, will help you learn how to create the user interface and start writing C# scripts to create player movements and artificial intelligence.

Chapter 7, Creating Levels and Game Progression, will help you learn how to create in-game power-ups to boost your player's ability and create save points to save your game progression.

Chapter 8, Post-Production and Visual FX, will show you how to enhance your game's visual quality by learning how to apply camera effects to your game and create numerous types of particle effects.

Chapter 9, Deploying the Game, will help you learn how to deploy your game for multiple types of platform with Unity.

What you need for this book

You need the latest version of Blender and Unity, preferably on Windows operating system, but both programs will also work on Mac OS X.

Who this book is for

This book is primarily for beginners who have just started to learn how to create their own games from scratch using free tools available on the Internet. This book also targets those who have had experience in developing games but have used some other expensive tools, such as Autodesk Maya, 3D Studio Max, and so on.

Conventions

In this book, you will find a number of styles of text that distinguish between different kinds of information. Here are some examples of these styles, and an explanation of their meaning.

Code words in text, database table names, folder names, filenames, file extensions, pathnames, dummy URLs, user input, and Twitter handles are shown as follows: we execute `GotoMainMenu()` by using the `StartCoroutine()` function, which "We will declare later."

A block of code is set as follows:

```
void Start ()
{
  mainMenuUI.SetActive (true);
  startGameUI.SetActive (false);
  exitGameUI.SetActive (false);
  newGameUI.SetActive (false);
}
```

When we wish to draw your attention to a particular part of a code block, the relevant lines or items are set in bold:

```
public void BackMainMenuPressed()
{
    selectedMode = mode.mainMenu;

    pauseMenuUI.SetActive (false);
    confirmUI.SetActive (true);
}
```

New terms and **important words** are shown in bold. Words that you see on the screen, for example, in menus or dialog boxes, appear in the text like this: "Then, set the AO map layer's **Blend** mode to **Multiply**."

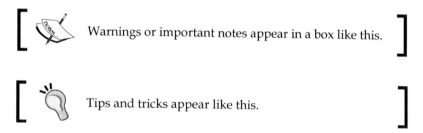

> Warnings or important notes appear in a box like this.

> Tips and tricks appear like this.

Reader feedback

Feedback from our readers is always welcome. Let us know what you think about this book—what you liked or may have disliked. Reader feedback is important for us to develop titles that you really get the most out of.

To send us general feedback, simply send an e-mail to `feedback@packtpub.com`, and mention the book title via the subject of your message.

If there is a topic that you have expertise in and you are interested in either writing or contributing to a book, see our author guide on `www.packtpub.com/authors`.

Customer support

Now that you are the proud owner of a Packt book, we have a number of things to help you to get the most from your purchase.

Downloading the color images of this book

We also provide you a PDF file that has color images of the screenshots/diagrams used in this book. The color images will help you better understand the changes in the output. You can download this file from: `http://www.packtpub.com/sites/default/files/downloads/Building_a_Game_with_Unity_and_Blender_ColorImages.pdf`.

Errata

Although we have taken every care to ensure the accuracy of our content, mistakes do happen. If you find a mistake in one of our books—maybe a mistake in the text or the code—we would be grateful if you could report this to us. By doing so, you can save other readers from frustration and help us improve subsequent versions of this book. If you find any errata, please report them by visiting `http://www.packtpub.com/submit-errata`, selecting your book, clicking on the **Errata Submission Form** link, and entering the details of your errata. Once your errata are verified, your submission will be accepted and the errata will be uploaded to our website or added to any list of existing errata under the Errata section of that title.

To view the previously submitted errata, go to `https://www.packtpub.com/books/content/support` and enter the name of the book in the search field. The required information will appear under the **Errata** section.

Piracy

Piracy of copyright material on the Internet is an ongoing problem across all media. At Packt, we take the protection of our copyright and licenses very seriously. If you come across any illegal copies of our works, in any form, on the Internet, please provide us with the location address or website name immediately so that we can pursue a remedy.

Please contact us at `copyright@packtpub.com` with a link to the suspected pirated material.

We appreciate your help in protecting our authors, and our ability to bring you valuable content.

Questions

You can contact us at questions@packtpub.com if you are having a problem with any aspect of the book, and we will do our best to address it.

1
Creating Your Game Concept

In this chapter, you will learn about the process of creating your game concept. It's usually called the **preproduction stage** where designers will plan out all of the game details ahead of time, that is, before entering the production stage where developers, such as programmers and artists, will start doing their works based on the game concept provided to them.

In this chapter, we will cover the following topics:

- Job roles in game development
- The gameplay design
- Writing the game's story
- Choosing a visual style
- The characters' concept
- The environment concept

Job roles in game development

Before we dive into the process of creating a game, let's take an overview on some of the roles in game development. We are looking at the general level, where each of these roles can be further split down into more specialized roles:

- **Game designer**: A game designer is a mastermind who designs the core elements and gameplay mechanics of a game. They not only need to understand how to design an interesting and fun game, but they also must have the creative and technical capabilities to communicate with the artists and programmers in order to make sure that both the artistic and technical processes comply with the game design.

- **Scriptwriter**: A scriptwriter is someone who helps to construct compelling scenarios and dialogues for in-game cinematics based on the storyline and direction set by the game designer. A good scriptwriter knows how to make the players emerge into the game world through storytelling techniques and esthetic wordings.

- **Programmer**: A programmer is a technical person who implements game features that run and control the game, as well as develop tools for the team to speed up the development process. They know every single bit of what's happening behind the game and occasionally turns coffee into code, too. Some of the specialized roles of a game programmer are a gameplay programmer, a toolkit programmer, a network programmer, a graphics programmer, and so on.

- **Artist/Animator**: A game artist is a creative person who designs and creates art assets for a game, such as concept arts, 3D models, textures, sprite sheets, particle effects, and so on. A game animator specializes in creating animations for the game characters as well as producing the in-game cinematics.

- **Audio engineer**: An audio engineer is an expert in creating the soundtrack for a game, including music, sound effects, character voices, and ambient effects. The audio engineer must be able to get the feel of the atmosphere of the game and create a suitable soundtrack accordingly.

- **Tester**: A game tester helps to playtest the game during the development phase to ensure that it's free of a programming bug and complies with the requirements set by the publisher. They will also make sure that the gameplay meets the expectation of the game designer and that it's fun to play with.

There are many other job roles that we have not covered here, such as an AI designer, a level editor, a lighting artist, and so on. Specialized roles like these are normally only available in big studios, which have the resources to ensure that every aspect of the game they are creating is at its highest standard.

For a smaller game development team, an individual team member can handle multiple roles, and more than one person can share some roles in order to split the workloads.

Gameplay design

The process of gameplay design can be divided into five major stages.

Starting point

Different people have different approaches in designing a game. Some designers like to start with the characters' design or storyline, and only after that, they will decide what type of gameplay is suitable for it. On the other hand, some designers like to start with the gameplay instead. There is no absolute rule on how to start designing a game; it's entirely dependent on what inspires you in the first place: Did a good story suddenly pop up in your mind? Were you inspired by a game you loved to play during childhood? Or were you inspired through silly conversations with your best friends? Write down your initial ideas; who knows, it could become the next popular game one day.

For me, I like to start by choosing the game genre and designing the gameplay right before anything else. I find that it's quite important to design a gameplay early on so that it can be tested repeatedly and to check whether the gameplay is fun or not. Otherwise, all the time we spent on writing a good storyline might be wasted if only to find out the gameplay simply doesn't work the way we had imagined. You can try to experiment on different approaches and see which method suits you more.

One mistake made by most of the newbie game developers is neglecting the importance of a **game design document (GDD)**. A GDD is usually a collaborative effort within a development team to organize ideas and help convey the designer's vision to the rest of the team. It also helps to make sure that everyone is working together at the same page, avoiding assumptions, and conflicting workflows.

Besides this, GDD is also very helpful for solo developers. It allows you to see the bigger picture of your game and easily spot any major flaws in the game design. Other than this, you can also look at the list of every aspect of the game and decide what needs to get done based on its priority.

Most of the time, a common office suite, such as Microsoft Office, OpenOffice, or LibreOffice, is sufficient for creating the GDD. If you're in a team, however, it's best to use an editor that has the capability of real-time collaboration between team members. I personally find Google Documents very useful for this purpose, especially during brainstorming sessions where every team member can contribute their ideas and let others to see them during discussion. Try to pick the most suited tool for you and your team.

Choosing a game genre

Picking a game genre early on is also very important. It gives you a sense of direction, and it lays down the foundation for you to further improve and innovate. There are many different types of game genres, such as first person shooter, role-playing, real-time strategy, adventure, action, and puzzle.

Alternatively, you may also *invent* your own genre if you are the type of person who likes to try out new ideas and always think out of the box. Although this may sound overly ambitious, but this is actually doable, as game genres are being *invented* all the time. However, following this path requires a ton of prototyping to prove that your idea is workable and fun as you're trying to create something that no one has even seen before.

If you have no idea which genre to pick at the moment, you might want to look at the statistics of the best-selling video game genres, and hopefully it will give you some inspiration:

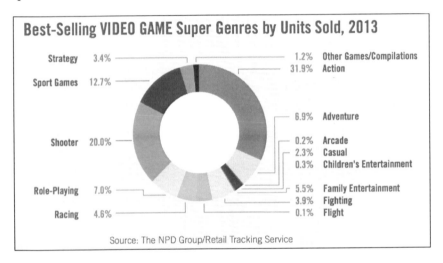

It's important to decide on the genre early before you start working on the game. Basically, switching game genres during development means starting all over again from scratch.

Game mechanics

Gameplay is something that connects players' actions with the purpose of the game and its main challenges. Gameplay will define what the player can or cannot do in the game, as well as conditions that allow the player to progress through the game. Gameplay design involves a wide range of designing aspects, such as a level design, gameplay balancing, player behavior prediction, and choices planning. All of this can be incorporated into something called **game mechanics**.

Game mechanics are constructs of rules that make up the gameplay of a game. It determines what actions the player can take, how the actions interact with the game states, and how other game entities respond to the player's actions. Gameplay defines what a game is to the player, whereas game mechanics are the parts that define the gameplay itself. In other words, gameplay is nothing more than a set of game mechanics. Oftentimes, gamers are popularizing famous games for its game mechanics. For example, Gears of War was famous for its cover mechanic when it first released in 2006. Prince of Persia blew peoples' minds away when first showing two of its famous mechanics — the parkour mechanic as well as the time manipulation mechanic. Angry Birds would not have been downloaded by two billion times across the globe if it didn't feature the slingshot mechanic!

We can split a set of game mechanics into two main categories: core mechanics and sub-mechanics. Core mechanics are the most important mechanics in your game. You cannot simply change your game's core mechanics because it will break the nature and essence of your game. For example, take away the shooting mechanic from Counter Strike, and the game would simply become something else, but something other than Counter Strike. It will not make any sense at all to play Counter Strike without a shooting mechanic. Sub-mechanics, however, can be taken away without breaking the game. Again, we use Counter Strike as an example, but this time, we will take away just the jumping mechanic. Now the players can no longer jump, but that doesn't make Counter Strike a different game; it's still a first person shooter, you can still make the headshots. It's important to determine what are the core mechanics of your game early on, but not so important for sub-mechanics. You can add in sub-mechanics later on during the production stage because, as previously mentioned, it won't break the game. A strong and solid core mechanics will ensure the success of your game, so focus on it first before anything else. After this, you can try to experiment on different sub-mechanics to enhance the gaming experience.

In short, proper planning will ensure that the gameplay is balanced, unpredictable, and makes sense to the player. Even an experienced game designer can hardly design a perfect gameplay in one shot. It takes a ton of testing and iterations in order to get the gameplay to feel right and fun to play with. The formula is simple: test, test, and more tests!

Level design

A level is the venue where a player interacts with the gameplay elements. It can also be called as a map or stage. As a level designer, you're responsible for designing the layout of the levels to comply with the purposes of your gameplay: Does this level carry missions? Is this level for multiplayer purposes? Roughly how long do you expect the user to play this level? You need to ask yourself all sorts of questions before you start designing your level.

One important aspect of level design is flow control. Game level with good flow control can direct a player toward the goal of the level and prevent idling or moments of unintentional confusion from occurring in game. You need to be clear about the intent and purpose of the particular level and then by using the elements within the level, such as lighting, props, and items. You can subconsciously lead the player toward the goal. You will learn more about this later when we design the environment.

Let's have a look at the sample level I designed for this book. Players must search for the key in order to open the gate and fight the final boss. While exploring the environment, player will occasionally encounter monsters and involve in intensive battles. There are also some items aligned randomly across the path for the player to pick up, restore health, and help progress the game. Here's an image showing a simple level with simple gameplay in mind to demonstrate what a map layout looks like:

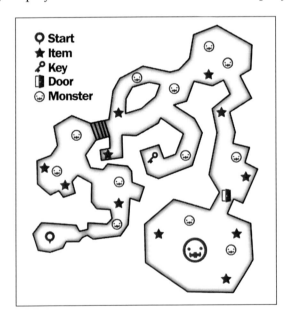

Rapid prototyping

Rapid prototyping is a good way to quickly test out your game idea and see if it works the way you want. Sometimes, a game idea might sound good only on paper, but it just doesn't work out like how you'd imagine it to be. The last thing you want is to only realize that you have been working on a bad idea in the middle of the development phase. Rapid prototyping not only saves you from this situation, but also allows you to think out of the box and freely experiment on all kinds of random ideas. If the idea works, then it is great; if it doesn't work, just scrap it and try the other ideas.

When you rapidly prototype your game, you should stop worrying about the graphics and just focus on the gameplay mechanics alone. The character could be just a cube, a sphere, or anything simple. The level could be just a plane or with more cubes on it acting as obstacles. You also shouldn't worry about the storyline at this stage because you might be scrapping the idea minutes later.

Unity Game Engine, the game development tool that we will be using in this book, is built for rapid prototyping in mind. It's extremely easy to just throw in some primitive shapes, applying some scripts to the shapes, and you are good to go. You can instantly start playtesting your ideas without much effort spent on setting up the game engine. In addition, you can download sample game assets from the Unity Asset Store, including 3D models, animations, and even sample scripts to kick-start your prototyping process.

Besides this, there are also plenty of plugins available at the Unity Asset Store, which provide extra tools for you to rapidly construct a demo level or create game mechanics without the need of writing any code. All-and-all, Unity Game Engine makes rapid prototyping even more rapid with the features mentioned previously. You will only be learning how to use Unity in later chapters.

Writing the game's story

Almost every video game has a storyline behind it. Even a game that has neither cinematic features nor a single line of dialogue could still contain a background story that defines the world of the game. Oftentimes, video game storyline is parallel to the progression of the gameplay. The further away the player progresses, the more they will learn about the storyline of the game.

You don't necessarily need to present your game's story through narratives or cinematic features unless you're making a story-heavy game, such as *Last of Us*. For a simple game, it's better to let the players discover the background story themselves by playing through your game. This is much more rewarding than directly telling them everything!

Choosing a visual style

Before we start designing the characters and environment, we need to set a visual guideline in order to ensure a consistent design throughout the game. When you place the characters together with the environment, they should fit with the background, and they should not have too distinctive art style and quality from each other as if the characters and environment were taken from different games.

Generally, visual style can be split between two categories: realistic and stylized. It's entirely up to you what type of style you want to pick for your game, whether it's ultrarealistic, extremely stylized, or somewhere in between. It depends on the vision you set for your game as well as your team's capability in delivering the art style. Discuss with your teammate what type of visual style they are comfortable with and make sure that you understand your team before you start, which will prevent a lot of troubles from happening during production stage.

The characters concept

The characters concept usually refers to the concept arts, which display the design of your game characters. Concept artists have to come out with dozens of sketches and color thumbnails before a final design is selected by the art director. Once the character concept is confirmed and finalized, 3D artists start working on the 3D models by referring to the concept arts provided for them.

It's not as difficult as you think to design a character from scratch. Make sure that you truly understand the game you're trying to make. If you don't, try to read through the GDD and the storyline repeatedly until you are very familiar with each character's background story, personality, and their roles in the game. Once you're familiar with the game characters, try to imagine how they should look like in the visual style you chose earlier.

When designing characters, it's best to start with the silhouette. Try to define the character's personality using only the silhouette and ignore all other forms of details. We don't need to worry about the color, texture, facial expression, clothing, accessory, and anything else at this stage. Focus only on the body shape, size, contour, and posture that can easily make a player recognize the character and be able to tell the roles of the characters by simply judging from its outlook.

I prepared an image showing three characters' silhouettes. Try to guess what their personality is by judging from their respective silhouette.

Let's take a closer look at this diagram:

- **Character A**: The first character looks small, cute, and vulnerable. He is probably harmless to you, don't you think so?

- **Character B**: The second character looks like an ordinary person, but his uneasy posture infers that he could be a sly character with bad intention. Better not to get too close to him.

- **Character C**: The third character looks extremely dangerous even from afar! Does he bite? I'm sure he does more than that!

Once you have chosen the silhouette of each character, you can now start adding detail! However, no color should be used at this stage. Use only lines to sketch out the appearance of the characters. Concept sketches should be fast, and it's okay for the sketches to look messy at this stage because we want our brain to continuously come out with different ideas without being distracted by small details. Don't be afraid to experiment with different ideas you have, you might be surprised how creative you could be!

After you've done a dozen or so rough sketches, pick one that you think most suitable for your game. Redraw the characters with fine lines and make sure that they look clean this time because we are going to put some colors on it!

The following image shows the sample characters' concept that I used for this book. I have chosen a more manga-ish, chibi style for my game characters. I skipped the silhouette and rough-sketching steps because well, the game demo I'm showing in this book is just a very, very simple game, so it's exceptional.

Now, let's take a closer look:

- **Character A**: Block out the character with simple shapes, only simple shapes!
- **Character B**: Start adding detail.
- **Character C**: Clean-up and finishing.

After you have done all the clean-up jobs, we will proceed to the next stage, which is adding colors to your characters! Use only plain colors to fill in the design at this moment. No lighting or shadow should be allowed because again, we want to focus on experimenting different sets of color pallets on our characters and not be distracted by elements.

Be cautious when deciding the color palette for your characters. Choosing the wrong color could influence your player's interpretation toward your character's personality and role. Wrong color could also affect the visual focus of your character, making it hard to be seen on the screen (for example, a green character standing on a grass field).

Here, I experimented with three different colors on my character. I picked the one that, in my opinion, resembles his personality:

- **Character A**: Although red color looks really nice on him, it looks way too aggressive and that doesn't suit my faint-hearted character.
- **Character B**: Blue color looks more calm and friendly, which is suitable for my character.
- **Character C**: Totally, not my cup of tea.

The same method is used for the monster design as well. Eventually, I picked the one with red/pink patterns on its body. The color is more aggressive and at the same time contradicts with the main character's color. Also, warm colors, such as red or orange, often represent caution or danger. In order to speed up the process, I will just pick monster C as the final boss.

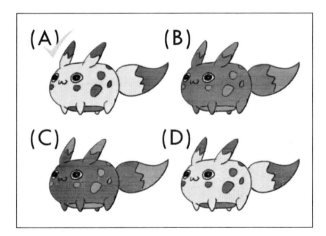

Finally, create a scale comparison chart to let everyone in your team know exactly how big or small should the characters look like. This information is extremely important for the 3D artists as well as gameplay designer. Make sure that everyone in your team is aware of this chart.

The environment concept

The environment concept, as the name implies, is the concept design for your game's environment. The difference between level design and environment design is that the latter is more about the art—how to use artistic elements to make the scene look more interesting. Many important guidelines will be given to the concept artists before they start using the environment concept. Artists need to know the visual style, color mood, detailed description of the environment, and most importantly, the level layout.

Here is the environment concept I did for this book. I split the layout into several parts and illustrated each of them based on the visual style and color mood I picked earlier. Note how I use lighting to guide player toward the correct path.

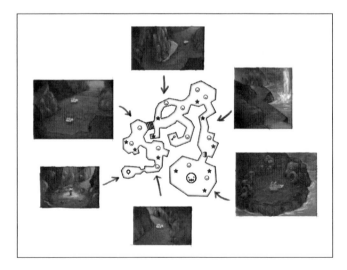

Summary

In this chapter, you learned all the important aspects on how to design your own game as follows:

- Introduction to important elements that you need to include in your game design, such as game genre, game mechanics, level design, storyline, and visual style
- Explaining what is rapid prototyping and how it helps establish a solid game idea
- The process of creating concepts for your game character and environment

In the next chapter, we will gain knowledge on how to turn our characters design into 3D models using Blender.

2
Creating Characters

In the previous chapter, we learned the process of creating our own game concept, which was mostly theoretical. In this chapter, however, we are going to get our hands dirty by learning how to create 3D characters from scratch using Blender!

In this chapter, we will cover:

- Downloading Blender for Windows, Mac OS X, or Linux
- A quick look at the basic user interface of Blender
- Creating a 3D model of the monster from scratch
- Unwrapping UV and creating a texture for the monster
- Creating a 3D model of the player character from scratch
- Unwrapping UV and creating a texture for the player character

Downloading Blender

As we all know, a blender is an electric kitchen appliance used to blend vegetables and fruits into drinks, sauces, or pastries. But in this tutorial, we will be using another Blender, which is an open source 3D computer graphics software developed and maintained by the Blender Foundation.

 You can download Blender for free, at http://www.blender.org/download.

Currently, three platforms are officially supported: Windows, Mac OS X, and Linux. Due to Blender's open source nature, it can be easily ported to other operating systems as well.

A brief history of Blender

Blender was originally proprietary software developed in the mid 90's by Ton Roosendaal for his animation company. Unfortunately, the company was shut down by investors in early 2002, resulting in Ton losing the ownership of Blender.

Later that year, Ton founded a non-profit organization called the Blender Foundation and successfully raised a total of 100,000 EUR in only seven weeks to convince the former company investors to agree on open-sourcing Blender.

On Sunday, October 13, 2002, Blender was released to the world under the terms of the GNU General Public License. Blender development has continued to thrive since that day, driven by an ever-growing team of dedicated volunteers from around the world led by Blender's original creator, Ton Roosendaal.

The basic user interface of Blender

After installing Blender to your computer, double-click on the Blender icon located either on the desktop or the Start menu to launch the program. You will see something like this once Blender is launched:

At the time of writing this book, the latest stable release of Blender is version 2.74. You might be seeing a different splash screen if you are using a different version of Blender, which is completely normal.

You can also switch off the splash screen by going to **File | User Preferences | Interface** and untick the **Show Splash** option.

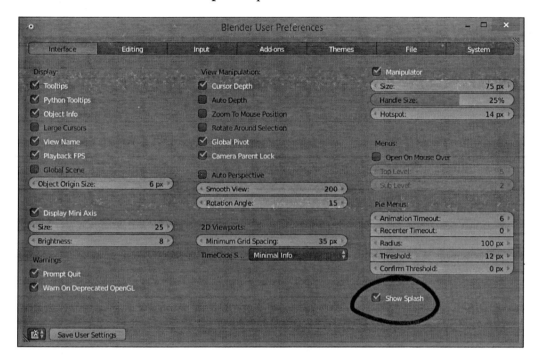

Blender has a completely unique user interface, which is quite different from any other 3D programs out there. Next I have labeled the panels that form the default Blender workspace and briefly explain what each of these panels is used for:

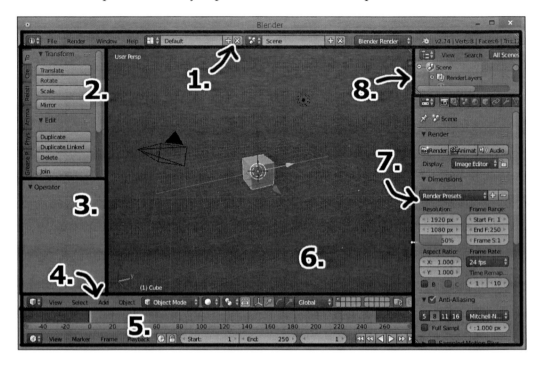

- **The Header menu** (1): The Header menu is a rectangular panel on the top that provides you with access to application-specific functions such as opening a project file, saving a file, importing/exporting data, user preferences settings, toggling the window full screen, and so on.

- **The Tool Shelf** (2): The Tools shelf is a panel containing shortcuts to frequently used operators such as buttons for creating and editing 3D meshes, animation, and physics tools, as well as quick access to the grease pencil.

- **The Operator window** (3): The **Operator** window displays properties related to an operation that you have just used, such as adding primitives, applying a rigid body to an object, and so on. If an operator does not have any properties, the **Operator** panel will be empty.

- **The 3D view menu** (4): The 3D view menu is where you can access menus related to the 3D view, such as adjusting the view and adding/selecting/manipulating objects in the scene. You will be using this menu all the time if you don't remember the shortcut keys.

- **The Animation timeline** (5): The Animation timeline is where you adjust your animation's key frames and curves. You can also find the **Playback** button here.

- **Main 3D view** (6): The main 3D view is a window that displays your 3D scene in real time for editing purposes. You will be doing all your work here.

- **The Properties window** (7): The Properties window displays the properties of the current selected object. You can also adjust the render settings here.

- **The Outliner window** (8): The Outliner window displays the list of objects in your 3D scene. You can select an object by simply clicking on it on the Outliner instead of selecting it in the main 3D view.

Blender's user interface is highly customizable, which means you can modify the workspace layout to fit your purposes. Every window can be moved, scaled, split, and combined. You will find a split-window widget either on the top-right corner or the bottom-left corner of every window. Clicking and dragging the widget inward will cause the window to split in half, whereas dragging it outward will make it combine with another window nearby. You can pick which window you want it to combine with by moving the mouse in different directions while holding the left mouse button. A big arrow will appear on the screen to indicate which window will be removed.

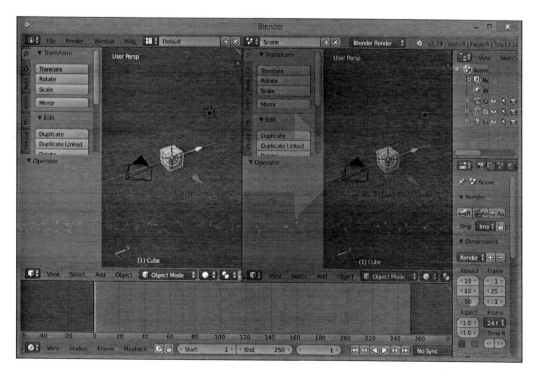

After you have customized your desired layout, you can save it by clicking on the + button besides the screen data block on the Header menu. You can easily switch between different layouts by choosing from the screen data block drop-down menu.

On the **Properties** window, you will see a row of buttons that look like this:

The icons will look different depending on the type of object selected in 3D view. Each of these buttons gives you access to a different context of the **Properties** settings, such as:

- **Render**: All the settings that control the rendering of the final images, such as the resolution, output format, performance, and so on.

- **Render layers**: Settings of each layer/render pass that get processed by the rendering engine to produce the final images.

- **Scene**: Here lie the settings for color management, camera choice for rendering, and units and gravity settings for physical modeling.

- **World**: These are the settings for the surrounding environment of which the models are rendered, such as background sky color, mist and star settings and environment lighting.

- **Object**: In here are settings that apply to all kinds of objects, such as transformations, layer assignments, and grouping. The settings shown here apply to the current selected object.

- **Object constraints**: These are the settings that limit the motion of the object for animation purposes. The limits can also be tied to the motion of other objects in various ways.

- **Object modifiers**: Modifiers are components that make changes to the geometry which only take effect at rendering time. Lamps, cameras, and empty objects can't have modifiers.

- **Object data**: Here you will find settings specific to the type of object: mesh vertex groupings, text font, lamp settings, camera settings, and so on. This is reflected in the icon, which changes according to the type of object selected.

- **Material**: The material settings for an object control how it looks: its color, whether it has a shiny or dull surface, how transparent it is, and so on.

- **Texture**: Textures are the graphical skins laid atop 3D models so they appear to have surface detail. The texture settings allow you to change the texture of a material or modify the properties of the texture.

- **Particle**: The **Particle** setting is used to change the way a set of particles behave, producing effects like smoke, flames, or sparks.

- **Physics**: Here you will find settings that control how the object reacts to forces like objects in the real world.

Most of these contexts are not really relevant to the game, so we can ignore them for the time being. Since we only use Blender for creating models and animations, we will only use the Object and Object modifiers settings most of the time.

 For more information regarding the user interface, you can check out Blender's user manual by going to **Help** | **Manual** on the Header menu and click on **Editors**.

Creating the monster's 3D model

In this chapter, we will be using the character concepts from the previous chapter to walk you through the process of constructing a 3D game character from scratch. Once you have learned how to do that, you can then try to draw your own concepts and turn it into a 3D model!

You may ask why we start constructing the monster first, and not the player character. The reason for this is because the body shape of the monster is much simpler compared to the player character. Constructing a humanoid 3D model is not the best way for a newbie to learn the basics of 3D modeling. We will come back to the player character once you have mastered the basic skills.

The first thing we need to do is to refer back to our monster concept art and try to imagine its body shape using just the combination of primitive geometries. This will help you see through the complexity of details such as texture, color, facial expression, and so on, and focus solely on the shape. This will help you in planning the steps needed to build the mesh.

Although most of the time a 3D model can be constructed from a cube, in this case (the preceding image) the monster's body is an oval shape and it's easier to build with a sphere. Therefore, the first thing we need to do is to delete the cube that is placed by Blender into the scene by default. First, select the cube by pressing the right mouse button. Next, click on the **X** key (or the *Delete* key) on your keyboard and a confirmation dialog will appear. Click on the **Delete** option on the dialog or press the *Enter* key to execute the delete operator. Now, the cube is gone. Hooray!

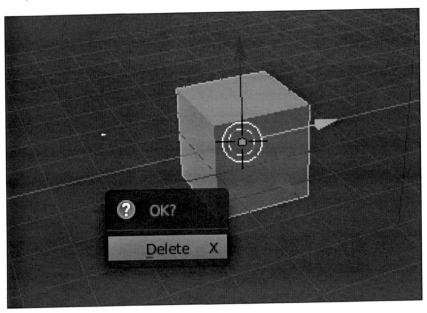

Unlike any other 3D programs, Blender uses the right mouse button for object selection instead of the left mouse button.

Now, you may have already noticed the little red-and-white striped circle with black crosshairs that changes its position whenever you left-clicked on the screen. It's called the 3D cursor, which is quite a unique feature not seen in any other 3D modeling tool. Most of the time, the 3D cursor is used for placement, whereby a newly created object will be placed exactly at the location of the 3D cursor. Besides that, it can also be used as the median point for translation, rotation, and scaling, as well as changing the pivot point of a mesh. You can read more about the usage of the 3D cursor in the Blender Reference Manual at `https://www.blender.org/manual/editors/3dview/3d_cursor.html`.

Next, we want to add a new object. To do that, you can either use the buttons in the Tools Shelf or simply press *Shift + A*. Select **UV Sphere** and now you will see a sphere that resembles a disco ball appearing in the scene. But before you do anything else, lower down the **Segments** and **Rings** values in the **Operator** window so that the number of polygons is reduced. You must do this right after the object is being created because you won't be able to set the properties again once you execute other operators.

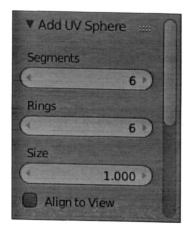

While the sphere is still being selected, go to the Tool Shelf and find the **Smooth** button under the **Shading** category. Click on the **Smooth** button and now you get a pretty-looking low polygon sphere that resembles a rock.

In order to look at your 3D model more closely and from all directions, you can use your mouse to navigate the 3D view. This, however, will only work if your mouse cursor is positioned within the 3D view's boundary. To zoom in and out from the view, scroll your mouse wheel accordingly; to rotate the view around the viewing point, hold the middle mouse button and move the cursor; to pan your view around, hold the *Shift* key and the middle mouse button at the same time and move the cursor. For more information, you can check out Blender's user manual by going to **Help | Manual** on the Header menu and search for **Navigating**.

Now, let's go back to the sphere we just created. We need to change the shape of the sphere to become slightly oval so that it matches our monster's body shape. There are many ways to manipulate the mesh, but I will teach you one of the fastest ways to do it—using shortcut keys. In this case, we want to scale the mesh along the *y* axis, so let's press the *S* key and then press the *Y* key. Now you can scale the mesh by simply moving your cursor. At this stage, however, the scaling is not applied to the mesh; you can either click on the left mouse button to apply the scaling, or cancel the operator by clicking on the right mouse button.

Do notice that the initial distance between your mouse cursor and the model when you initiate the scaling mode will affect the magnitude of scaling to your model. Try to put your mouse cursor slightly further away from the 3D model when you're about to press the S key, as that will give you a more natural scaling and it is easier for you to control it.

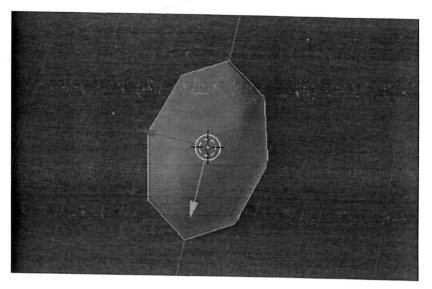

Next, what I'm going to do is to remove half of the model and ask Blender to mirror the other side of the model later. By doing this, you only need to edit half of the model and the other side will be automatically handled by Blender. This is only useful for 3D models that are symmetrical, such as humanoid characters and animals.

To remove the other half of the mesh, what we need to do is to keep the mesh selected and press the *Tab* key to enter the **Edit** mode. Once you're in the **Edit** mode, you can manipulate up to every individual polygon and every vertex. Next, press *A* to deselect the vertices and press *Z* to enter the wireframe mode. Then, adjust your view to the front of the mesh, press *B* to batch-select vertices, and select half of the model.

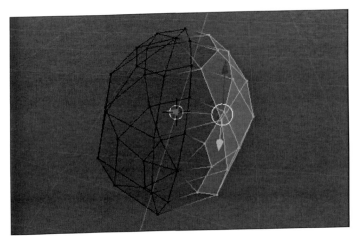

After that, press *X* and select **Vertices** from the menu that pops up. You will now get a half-spherical object that looks like the one in the following screenshot. Press the *Z* key to turn off wireframe mode and press *Tab* again to return to object mode.

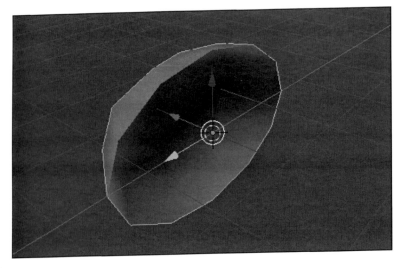

To mirror the 3D model, exit the Edit mode and go to the modifier tab at the
Properties window. Click on the **Add Modifier** drop-down menu and choose
Mirror under the **Generate** category. The mirror modifier will automatically
generate identical but flipped geometries of the object the modifier is attached to,
along the axis set by the user. Do notice that all the modifiers are non-destructive
effects, meaning as long as you have not clicked on the **Apply** button, the effect of
the modifier is not actually applied to your mesh yet, and you can easily change its
settings or remove it completely without harming your model. This, however, will
cost a bit more of your CPU power for Blender to display the previewing result of
the modifier.

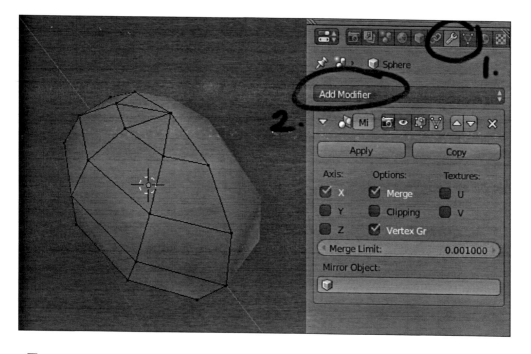

To save your working file in Blender, press *Ctrl + S*. If it is not
the first time you have saved, Blender will automatically create a
backup for your previous saved file. You will find an extra file with a
`.blend1` extension being generated alongside your latest saved file
that has the `.blend` extension.

Next, we will be adding legs to the monster. Enter Edit mode again, but this time, we want to select the faces instead of vertices. To do that, press *Ctrl + Tab* and select **Face**. Then, hold *Shift* and use the right mouse button to select four faces where we want the legs to *grow* on.

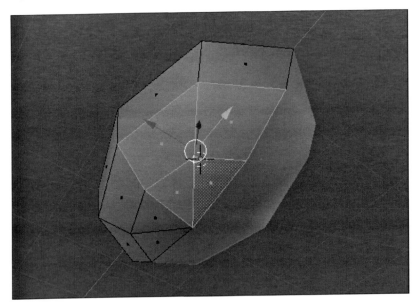

Next, press *E* to extrude the faces. But do not move the faces away from the original position; press the right mouse button to cancel the extrusion. Why? Because we wouldn't want a leg the size of an elephant! Even though you have canceled the extrusion, the faces have actually duplicated at the original position. Now, press *S* to scale down the duplicated faces to roughly half the original size. Before we extrude the faces again, try to adjust the vertices so that the surface looks smooth so that you get a good-looking mesh from the extrusion.

It's always a good practice to make sure the model looks fine before moving to the next steps. This is because every small mistake accumulated along the way may result in more problems in a later stage, which may cause frustration when you are trying to fix those issues that could be avoided in the first place.

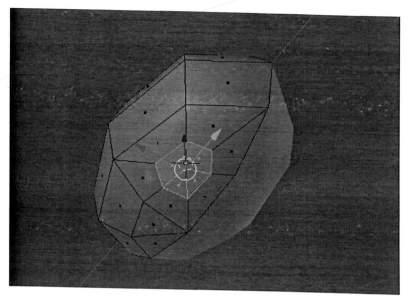

Once you are ready, press *E* again to grow the leg! Now you will notice that the other half of the body is mimicking exactly what you're doing; that's the mirror modifier doing its job. This way, you will be twice as productive and won't worry about the model not being symmetrical.

After you have extruded the leg, scale down the tip of the leg slightly and reposition the whole leg to the side. If we take real animals as a reference, we can notice their legs are not growing out from the chest, but rather from the shoulders and hips that are located at the side of the body. Usually this takes some time to adjust but it will make your life easier later on because it will be extremely hard to change the structure of the model once it's getting more complex in a later stage.

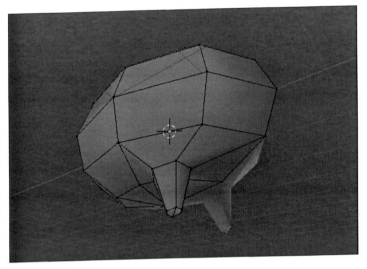

The leg currently looks very straight and rigid, so let's add more lines to it by pressing *Ctrl + R* for initiating the loop cut operator. You will now see a pink line appearing whenever you move your cursor around the 3D model. Move your cursor to the area between the thigh and the tip of the monster's leg, then press the left mouse button to confirm the cutting. After that, scale it slightly bigger to make the leg look bulkier.

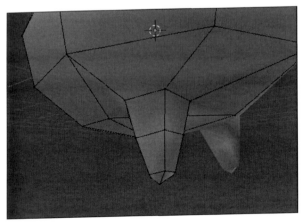

Repeat the same steps to create the other legs. With all four legs sticking out from the body, it's now starting to look like a living creature instead of a rock!

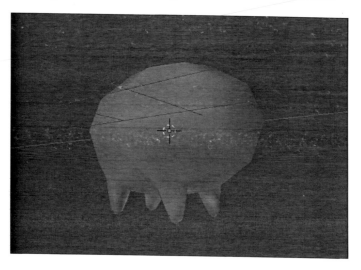

Next, we will do the bunny ears. Just like what we did previously, again, we select a face that we want the ear to be extruded from. Extrude it once at the original position and scale it down slightly.

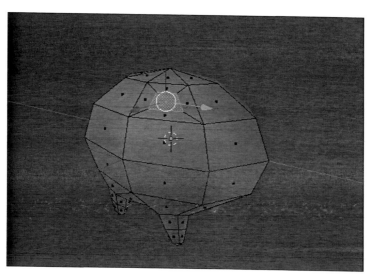

Once you are happy with its size and shape, press *E* again to extrude from it. This time, make it really long so that it matches the length shown in the concept art.

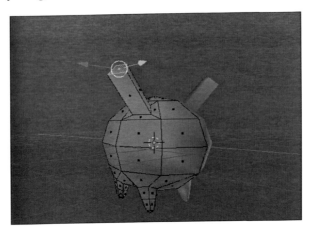

 If you extruded a surface but never moved it away, you will be getting duplicated geometries that may cause problems later. To remove duplicated geometries, select all the faces/edges/vertices of the model, press the *W* key and select **Remove Double** from the menu. Blender will automatically detect the doppelgangers and remove them.

Then, like what we did previously to the leg, we make a loop cut in the middle of the ear by pressing *Ctrl* + *R*. Once you've done that, adjust the shape of the ear until it looks like the concept art.

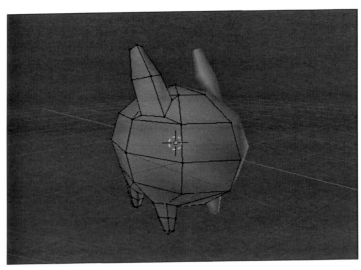

Now let's move on to the last part—the tail. You might think the shape of the tail is very difficult to construct, since it has a non-uniform shape and appears to be very curvy. However, try to recall what I told you previously when I mentioned how the body shape of the monster can actually be formed by using just primitive shapes. We are actually going to do that now—let's create a primitive shape.

Have you noticed the small cursor that seems to do nothing but keep changing position whenever you mistakenly press the left mouse button? It's called the 3D cursor, a multi-purpose movable pivot point that I find very useful from time to time. You can rotate an object around the 3D cursor, or change an object's center of origin to where it's positioned, or any other operators that require position data. In this case, we want to create a sphere behind the monster, so let's move our mouse cursor to somewhere behind the monster and press the left mouse button.

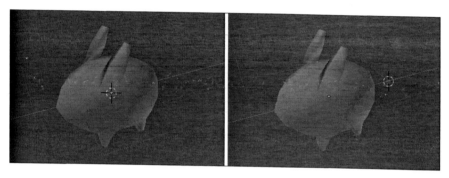

Although now it appears to be positioned behind the monster, when you move your view around you will notice it's actually not positioned exactly there. To solve this problem, we will use the snapping operator by pressing *Shift + S* and choose **Snap Cursor to Grid**. If you can't remember all the shortcut keys, you can press the space bar and search for the function you're looking for. For example, I type the word snap and all the operators related to it will appear on the menu, including the one I was using—**Snap Cursor to Grid**.

Once you have created the sphere, set the value of **Segments** to 8 and that of **Rings** to 6 to keep the polygon low. Now, rotate it 90 degrees along the *x* axis by pressing *R* and then *X*, and then type 90 on the keyboard. It's basically a combo shortcut key that makes the process really quick.

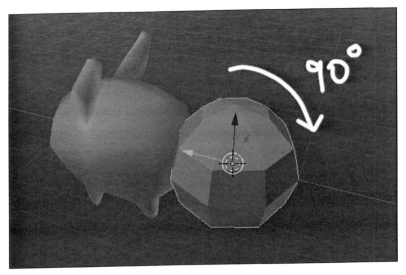

After that, select the faces at the back of the sphere and extrude it outward.

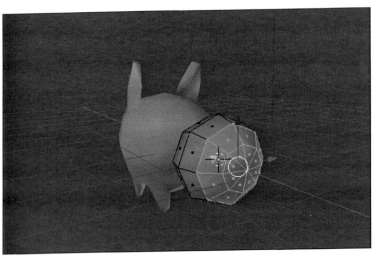

Then, rotate the faces along the *x* axis to make it face up.

Adjust the tip of the sphere until it looks pointy.

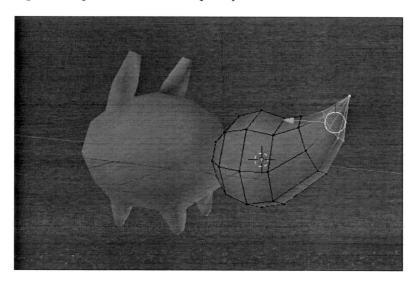

Lastly, add a loop cut to make the curve look more even and smooth. After that, you can join both the body and tail meshes together into one, by pressing *Ctrl + J*.

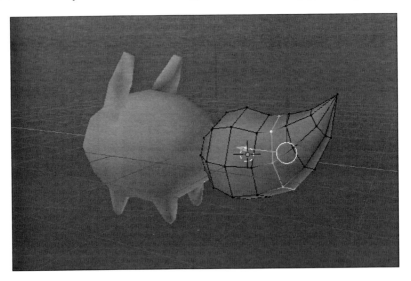

There we have it! The monster's model is now completed. You might find some small problems here and there later on but that's fine. It's completely normal to have tons of iterations along the way.

Unwrapping the monster's UV map

UV mapping is the process of converting the texture space of the 3D mesh into a 2D representation so that a texture can later be applied correctly.

To unwrap our monster's UV map in Blender, we need to first open up the UV editor window. Click and drag the split-window widget located in the top-right corner of your 3D view to split open a new window. Choose **UV/Image Editor** from the editor type drop-down menu and now you will see the UV editor alongside your 3D view.

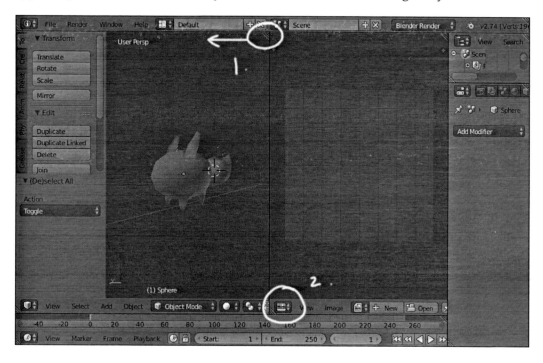

The first step to UV unwrapping is to find out where to cut out the seams. First, select the edges that connect the ears and legs to the body.

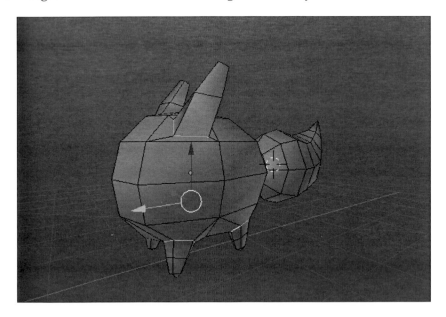

Then, press *Ctrl + E* to open up the menu containing all operators related to edges. Click on **Mark Seam** to tell Blender to cut these edges when we unwrap the UV map. The edges will then be marked with thick red lines.

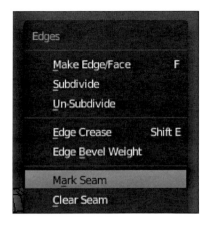

After that, mark all the other seam lines with the same method. Try to mark the edges that are hard to notice from the player's view so that any visual artifacts that might happen along the seam lines can be well hidden. Next I have highlighted the seam lines that I applied to the monster using white lines so that you can refer to it. Notice how I try to flatten the face UV as much as possible to minimize texture distortion on the face.

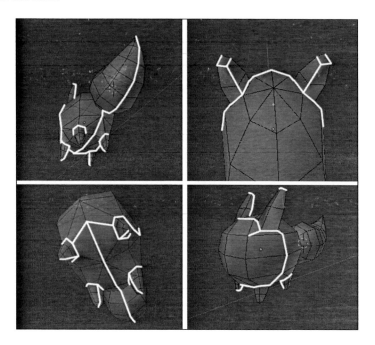

When you're done marking the seam lines, press *U* and select **Unwrap**. Blender will automatically unwrap the UV map based on the seam lines that you set beforehand. However, it's not done yet.

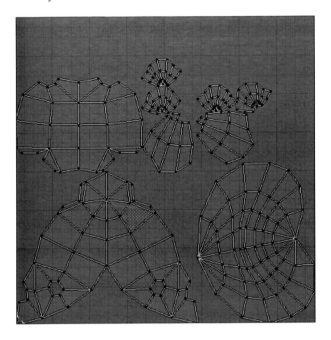

We need to check whether the UVs are being unwrapped correctly by using a checker texture. Under the UV editor window, click the **+ New** button and a dialog box will appear. Change the **Generated Type** option to **UV Grid** and click on **OK**.

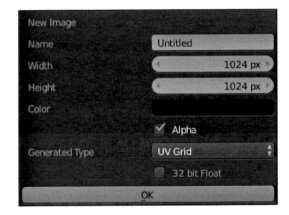

A checker texture will now be applied to your 3D model, but you still won't be able to see it until you change the 3D view's **Viewport Shading** option to **Texture** mode.

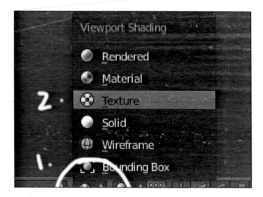

You will now see the checker texture being wrapped around the monster. This way, any distortions can be noticed and fixed easily. If the distortions happen at the area that can hardly be noticed by the player, then it's OK to just ignore it provided it's not causing any serious artifacts.

After that, we will arrange the UV islands so that it occupies most of the empty spaces on the texture. The first thing I usually do is to move all the UV islands outside the map area and slowly move it inside the map one by one. It's proven to be quite a clean and efficient way to arrange UV islands because you won't get distracted by other islands while doing the placement.

UV editing in Blender is exactly the same as editing a 3D model: right-click on the area to select a point, press *B* to batch select, *G* to move things around, *R* for rotation, *S* for scale, and so on. The workflow remains unchanged even though we're in a different type of window doing a different task.

It may take some time to properly arrange all the UV islands. While doing it, you might find issues related to the seam lines and require a re-unwrap. Try to correct the UV as much as possible at this point to avoid problems occurring during the texturing stage.

The following screenshot shows the final UV map for the monster. We can now export the UV map by clicking on the **UVs** menu below the UV editor window and choose **Export UV Layout**. Export the UV map to your computer and let's move on to texturing!

Creating the monster's texture

Once you're happy with the UV map, you can now remove the checker texture and replace it with a blank texture by clicking on the **+ New** button and pick **Blank as the Generated Type**. What I'm trying to do now is to bake the soft shadow that we usually call the ambient occlusion onto the blank texture. This AO map not only serves as a guideline for texture painting but also makes the final texture look more realistic. This step is not necessary depending on what style you're trying to do.

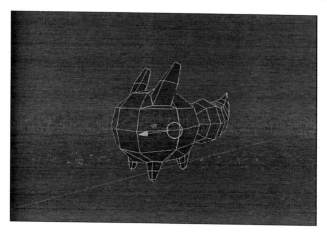

On the **Properties** window, switch over to the **World** tab and check **Ambient Occlusion**. Then, scroll down a little bit and you will see the **Gather** category. Change the **Samples** value from **5** to **15**.

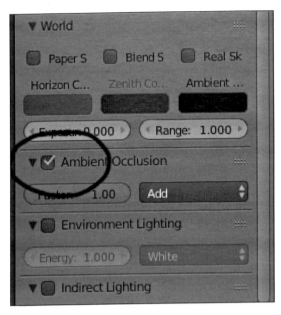

Next, go to the **Render** tab and open up the **Bake** category. Change **Bake** mode to **Ambient Occlusion** and check **Normalized**. The normalized setting will make the AO map look brighter and clean.

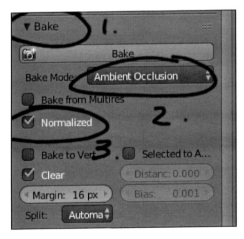

Once you're done with the settings, click on the **Bake** button and watch the magic happen!

Although the ambient occlusion now looks pretty good, there are some noticeable artifacts. This happens because the mesh is too low-polygon for Blender to bake the AO correctly. To solve this issue, we need to temporarily increase the polycount for baking the AO map, and then reduce it back to the original polycount. Sounds scary? You can actually achieve that using Blender's Subdivision Surface modifier.

While the mesh is selected, switch over to the **Modifier** tab and click on **Add Modifier**. From the drop-down menu, select **Subdivision Surface** to apply the modifier to the monster. Set the **Subdivision** settings to 4 and uncheck **Subdivide UVs**. We want to increase the polygon and not affect our UV map. Blender's modifiers are non-destructive to your mesh, which means it will keep a copy of your original mesh in the memory and can be recovered anytime by removing the modifiers from the mesh, as long as you don't click on the **Apply** button on the modifier.

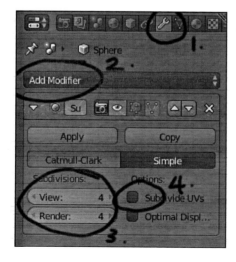

After you have applied the subdivision modifier to the monster, try to bake the AO map again. This time, you will get a much better ambient occlusion that looks nice and clean. The subdivision modifier can then be removed from the mesh by clicking on the **X** button on its top-right corner. To export the AO map, simply go to **Image** | **Save as Image** on the bottom of your UV/Image Editor.

Open up your image editing software that support multilayer editing, such as Photoshop, GIMP, Sumo Paint, Krita, and so on. Then, place the UV map and AO map into a different layer so that you can easily turn it on and off when you're creating the texture. Set the ambient occlusion layer's blending mode to **Multiply** so that it will blend with the texture layers below it.

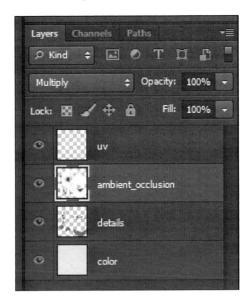

And finally, the texture is ready!

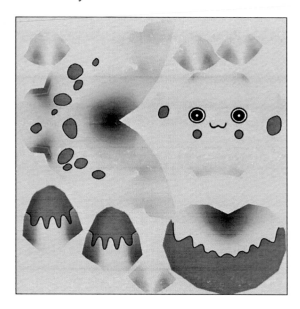

To apply the texture onto the mesh, click on **Image** and choose **Open Image** from the UV editor menu. Pick the texture you have just created and there you have it.

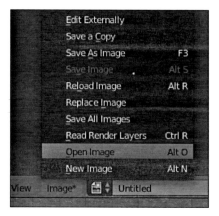

Notice how the flat UV on the face area makes the texturing process easier. The eyes and mouth appear to match exactly the texture because there aren't any stretches on the UV. This is why you should always put more effort into UV unwrapping to avoid problems during the texturing stage. We have completed the monster model. Hip hip hooray!

 Blender's material system is not used when creating 3D assets for game engines other than the **BGE** (**Blender Game Engine**). Other game engines are using their own distinctive material system, hence it's not possible to export Blender's materials to these game engines. Instead of using the materials in Blender, textures are opened directly in the UV/Image Editor for preview purposes.

Creating the player character's 3D model

Now that you are equipped with all the basic modeling skills, let's move on to create the player character. Phew, we have come such a long way!

Although a humanoid character tends to look very complicated, if we take away the details and just look at its simplified form, what we will see is a bunch of cylindrical shapes stuck together with a spherical head on top.

That is exactly what we are going to do next—create a bunch of cylinders and a sphere at a low segments count; I usually go for 6-8 segments so it's easier to edit. Then, arrange the cylinders and sphere nicely so that it look like a stickman.

Next, join all the shapes together into one single object by pressing *Ctrl + J*. Then, delete the other half of the model (only the body part, not the head) and apply the mirror modifier to make our lives easier. Do note that if your object's pivot point is not in the middle, your model will look extremely wrong when the mirror modifier is applied.

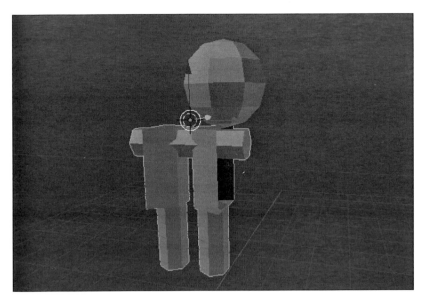

To solve this problem, place the 3D cursor at the center of the grid and click on **Set Origin** followed by **Origin to 3D Cursor** on the Tool Shelf. What this does is change the pivot point of the mesh to where the 3D cursor is located. The mirror modifier uses the mesh's pivot point to calculate where to generate and position .the mirrored twin.

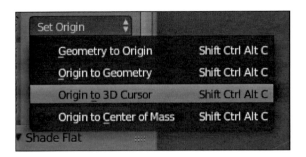

After that, we need to delete the faces hidden between the cylinders so that later we can merge the cylinders together by welding the vertices.

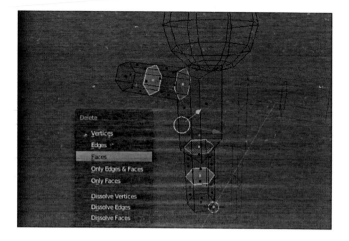

Press *Ctrl + R* to make a loop cut around the upper body. Then, make another loop cut in the middle as we are going to make a hole for the arm to connect to the body.

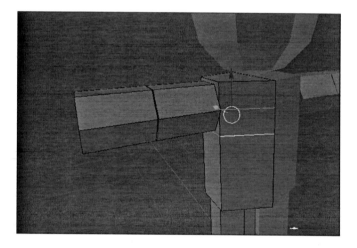

Next, we will merge all the parts together by welding the vertices together. Select two or more vertices and press *W* followed by choosing **Merge** from the menu, and then choose **At First/At Last/At Center/At Cursor** to execute the merge operator.

Once you are done merging the vertices, make a few more loop cuts around the model in preparation for modeling the knees and elbows.

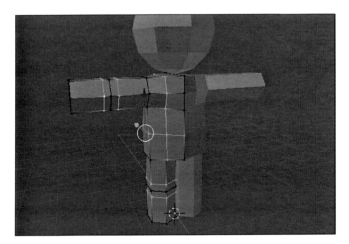

Create the knees by joining some of the vertices together and then manually move the vertices until the leg looks something like this:

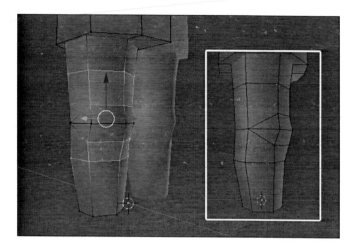

After that, repeat the same steps to create the shape of the arm.

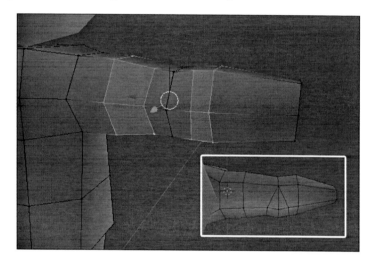

Once you're happy with the legs and arms, we will move on to create the character's head. The shape of a humanoid head is much more complex than other parts of the body. If we look into a mirror, we will realize that our head is in fact more than just a sphere, because there is something called a *face* growing out from the sphere, like so:

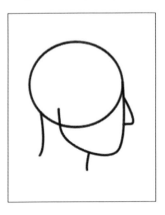

However, since we are making a low-polygon model, it's simply impossible to replicate the complicated shape of our face. What we can do, however, is to emulate the shape through approximation. In fact, we are going to just move a few vertices in front to make it look like the face of a wrapped mummy.

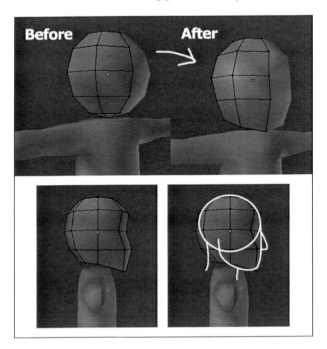

Next, adjust the vertices at the bottom of the head. Leave some space for the jaws and the rest is for the neck.

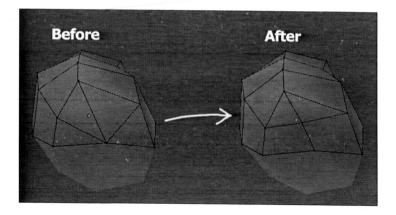

Extrude the neck out from the head and weld the vertices to the body. Don't forget to delete any faces that are hidden within the inner side of the model.

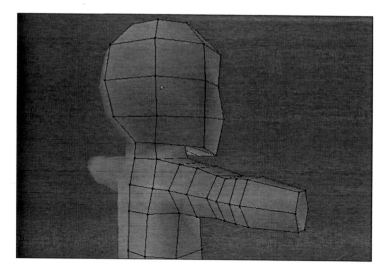

After that, connect both the legs together by creating the pubis using extrusion. Make sure the **Clipping** option is checked on your mirror modifier so that the vertices will not cross to the other side.

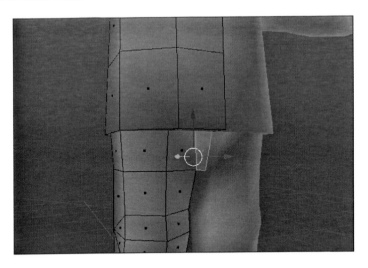

Next, we will create the feet through a combination of loop-cutting and extrusion. First, make a loop cut at the bottom of the leg. Then, extrude the faces in front followed by merging the top vertices with the bottom to make it look like a foot.

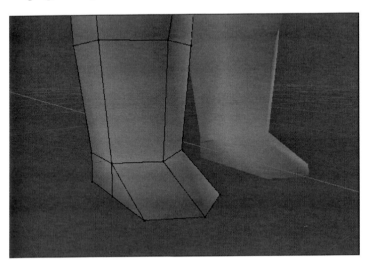

Once you're done with that, extrude the front part of the arm several times and manually adjust the shape of the fist. If you're unsure about what a fist looks like, try to look at yours!

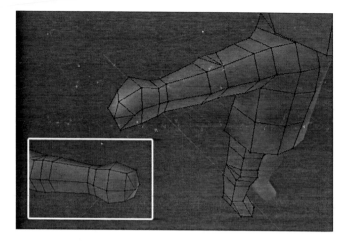

Then, we will create the sleeve using extrusion. Try to separate the vertices of the arm that connect to the shirt. It will cause Z-fighting problems later in the game.

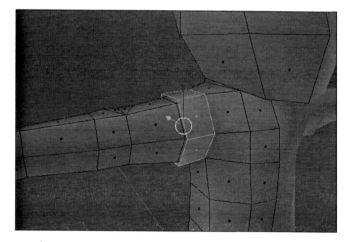

 Z-fighting is a visual artifact that occurs when two or more polygons are occupying the same space, causing the polygons to *fight* among themselves to determine who should be rendered on the screen, resulting in a flickering effect.

Next, we will create the hem of the shirt. This part requires more work as the shape is much more complicated. Try not to use a transparent texture for this purpose, or should I say, try not to use any transparent textures in your game whenever possible. That's because transparency sorting requires comparing the depth between each pixel, which will impact the performance of your game; use it only at a minimum.

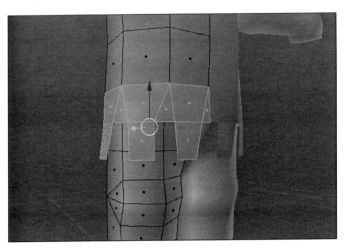

After you have done the hem, let's move on to the visor. It's a very simple shape that can be done using a plane. Create a plane by pressing *Shift + A* and select **Mesh** followed by **Plane**.

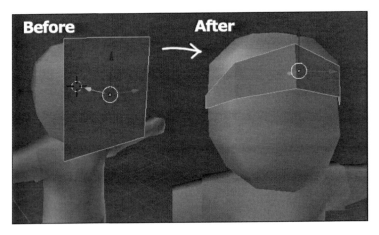

After that, create the pivot of the visor by simply adding a cylinder shape and scale it down.

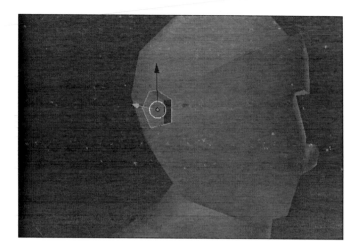

Next, we're going to create the ears. Just like how we did the ears of the monster, we first select the faces of the face (no pun intended) and extrude it one time without moving its position, then scale it down roughly to the size of an ear. After that, extrude it a few times and manually move the vertices to make it look like an ear. After the ear is done, I also adjusted the edges of the face to reduce shading distortion and make it look better.

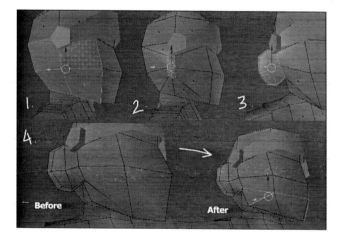

Then, we will be making the features on the helmet. This is also done using just planes.

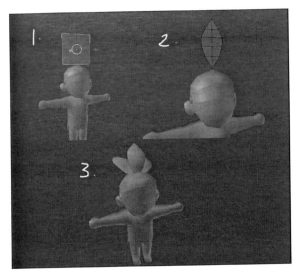

Next, I created a sword from a box using a combination of loop-cutting, extrusion, and moving vertices around.

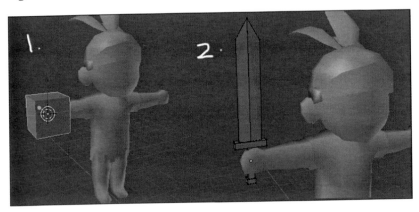

After a lot of time and effort, we finally get this splendid result!

Unwrapping the player character's UV map

Before we unwrap the UV map of the character model, we need to identify where to cut the seam lines so that the resulting UV will have minimum stretches, while effectively hiding the texture seams. Next I have highlighted the seams I marked on the character model using white lines. Since I used the mirror modifier on this model (except the feathers), most of the UV islands only appear in half, which means the other side of the mesh is sharing the exact UV space with the original mesh. This saves a lot of UV space, thus allowing us to enlarge all the UV islands that enable us to display the finer details of the texture.

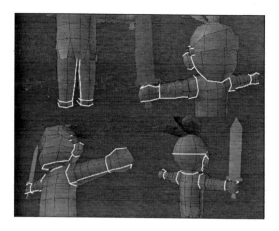

For this character, I'm more focusing on the face and torso's UVs because those areas have more important details than other parts of the mesh. I manually straighten the UVs of these two parts so that I can more easily create the texture without worrying about stretches and distortions. I wasn't too concerned about the other parts that have no details but only flat colors. Focus on the parts that really matter.

Before I start creating the texture for this character, I bake the ambient occlusion map just like we did previously when creating the monster's 3D model. Due to the complexity of this character in both the mesh structure as well as the shared UV map, quite a few visual artifacts occurred on the AO map. This, however, is not really a big issue as we can fix it later in the image editing software when creating the texture.

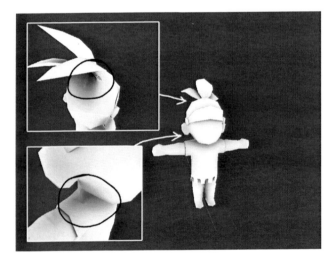

After that, put both the UV map and AO map into the image editing software and place them into separate layers. Then, set the AO map layer's **Blend** mode to **Multiply**. The rest is entirely up to your own creativity.

When I was working on the character's texture, I forgot the face and body are both mirrored and thus unable to draw the hair and sword belt onto the texture map. To solve this problem, I created the hair and sword belt using polygons instead, which turns out pretty well. The following is what the character looks like after applying the texture!

 To learn more about the hotkeys available in Blender, download the Blender Hotkey Reference document at the following link: http://download.blender.org/documentation/ BlenderHotkeyReference.pdf.

Summary

In this chapter, we have learned how to use Blender to build low-polygon 3D models from scratch. We have gone through the most important topics such as 3D modeling, UV unwrapping, and texturing, which enable us to create beautiful assets for any types of games.

In the next chapter, we will learn how to set up bones and rigs for our characters and start animating them.

3
Animating Your Characters

In this chapter, you will learn how to bring your characters to life by adding skeleton to them and creating animations, which will be used later for the game project.

In this chapter, we will cover the following topics:

- What is character rigging?
- Creating a monster's armature
- Creating a player character's armature
- Weight painting
- Animating characters

What is character rigging?

Rigging is the process of creating a custom-sized skeleton (which we refer as an armature), which will later be bidden into the character model through a process named **skinning**, to make its body parts movable. In AAA quality games, character rigs often contain more than just bones. For example, controllers are parented to groups of bones in order to animate them more easily, without directly touching the bones, but at the cost of spending more time in setting up the controllers.

Sometimes, constraint modifiers are also used when building a complex rig. However, such advanced features are not supported by all game engines. Therefore, game artists have to be really sure that their game engine supports these features before using them on their art assets.

Unity Engine does not import constraint modifiers from 3D modeling software. Therefore, it's not advisable to use constraints in your character rigs. If you do, however, you are required to bake the animation before exporting it to the FBX format. We'll look at this more in a later chapter.

Creating a monster's armature

We will start rigging our monster character by adding an armature into the scene. You can do this by pressing *Shift + A*, going to **Armature,** and clicking on **Single Bone**. This will create an armature set that contains only a single bone. Don't worry about it for now, as we can add more bones later on. Make sure that the armature is placed within the monster's mesh.

You will realize that you can hardly see the bone as it's now completely blocked by the mesh. Keep the armature selected, then go to the **Properties** panel under the **Armature** tab, scroll down to the **Display** section, and select the **X-Ray** option. The bone is now rendered in front of the mesh instead of being blocked by it. This allows you to edit the bones as well as animate the character with ease.

Next, we will start adding more bones to the armature. While the armature is being selected, press *Tab* to enter the Edit mode; you can now select, move, rotate, and scale individual bones just like you edit the 3D mesh. The first thing we need to do is to rotate the only bone around the *x* axis by 90 degrees. You can achieve this by selecting the individual bone and using the rotate manipulator to rotate it, or by using the shortcut key, which is much faster and flexible. Simply press *R*, press *X*, and type 90; you have now rotated the bone in lightning speed!

The first bone is often named the **root bone**. It is probably the only bone that has no parent, but it is linked by a chain of children bones. Thus, when you move the root bone, all the other bones will be moved along with it because the root bone sits on top of the chain hierarchy. Therefore, we will place the root bone somewhere in the middle of the mesh as when the animator moves or rotates the bone in the torso, it makes sense for the entire monster to move or rotate as well. On the other hand, it would not make any sense, for example, if the entire body rotates when the animator is just rotating the head bone.

To move the root bone, you can use the transformation manipulator or simply press the *G* key. Once you have positioned the root bone, select one of the small spheres at the tip of the bone and press *E* to extrude a child bone from it. Select the bone you have just extruded and press *E* again to extrude a child bone from it. Repeat this step several times until you get this:

At this point, we have created a chain of bones resembling the spine as well as the tail. We are about to create the bones of the limbs and ears, but we are not going to extrude them one by one as it's very time consuming and difficult to make the bones perfectly symmetrical on each side.

Just like what we did when we modeled the character mesh, we can mirror our armature with Blender as well, but not in the form of a modifier. The armature comes with an option named **X-Axis Mirror**. You can select this option in the **Options** tab on the Tools Shelf panel. You must enter the Edit mode while the armature is selected in order to see this option.

Once **the X-Axis Mirror** option is ticked, you can now extrude two bones simultaneously by pressing *Shift + E*. The other bone is the mirrored version and is thus is automatically positioned on the other side of the bone you just extruded. You can still extrude a single bone by pressing *E* without holding the *Shift* key. Play around with it until you get something like this:

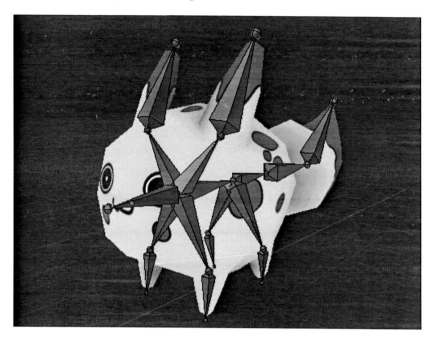

Next, we are going to bind the armature to the mesh using a process named **skinning**. To do this, quit the Edit mode and select the mesh. Then, hold *Shift* and select the armature. The selection order is very important—the armature must be the last selected object in order for this to work. Press *Ctrl + P*, and a menu with the title **Set Parent to** will pop out. Select **Armature Deform with Automatic Weights** and we're done.

What we actually did was ask Blender to automatically assign weights to the skin when binding the armature to the mesh. This usually only works well with a simple mesh, like the one we're working on now, and may cause problems with a more complicated mesh. The other options require a different setup, so we will ignore those for now.

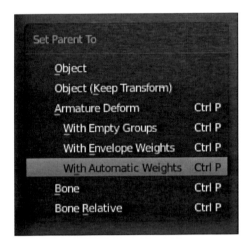

In order to test the rig, select the armature and enter Pose mode by choosing the **Pose Mode** option from the combo box, as shown in the following screenshot

 Keep in mind that the **Pose Mode** option is only available when an armature is selected, and it will not appear otherwise.

Once you're in Pose mode, you can freely move or rotate the bones around without actually affecting the original posture of the armature. If you try to go back to Edit mode, you will see all the bones returned to their original position and rotation. This allows you to edit your bones at any time in the middle of animating your character. Blender is such a flexible tool!

Move the bones around and make some poses to see whether any problems occur with the mesh deformation. For a simple mesh like this one, there are usually no major problems, and only a few very minor ones. You can come back to fix the minor problems once we have learned how to do skin weight painting. More details on this will be covered later in the chapter.

Creating the player character's armature

The process of creating the armature for the player character is very similar to that of the monster. The first thing we need to do is create a new armature by pressing *Shift* + *A*, followed by going to **Armature | Single Bone**. Next, place it somewhere around the hip, and not in the upper torso. This is where the center of mass lies in the human body, so it's most natural to place the root bone around that area.

After this, select one of the small spheres at the tip of the root bone and press *E* to create a child bone from it. Repeat the same step on the child bones until you get something like this:

Next, enable **X-Axis Mirror** and create bones for the limbs by pressing *Shift + E* to mirror-extrude the bones. Slowly adjust the bones until it look something like this:

After you have done creating all the bones for the character, we will now try to bind the armature to the character mesh using the same method as before. Press *Ctrl + P*; a menu will pop out. Now, select **Armature Deform with Automatic Weights**. This time, however, instead of successful binding of the armature to the mesh, you will get an error:

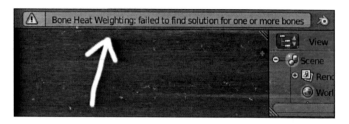

This happens because the character mesh is simply too complicated for Blender to automatically assign weights to the skin. Therefore, we can't use this method this time and we will require some manual labor to make it work. To do this, we need to first of all understand how skinning works.

Skinning is the process of attaching your character's mesh to the armatures you have created so that when one of the bones moves, the vertices of the mesh will also follow the movement of the bone. How does a vertex know which bone is associated with it? Well, the scaling factor has many names, often named **vertex weight**, **blend weight**, or **skin weight**. The higher the value of the skin weight of a vertex associated with a specific bone, the more it will be affected by the movement of that bone.

For example, if the skin weight of a vertex associated with a bone is at the factor of 1.0, it will move exactly like how the bone is moving. If the skin weight is 0.0, then the vertex will not move at all when the bone is moving. Likewise, if the skin weight is at the factor of 0.5, the vertex will only move half as much as the bone.

In Blender, the value of the skin weight is represented with different colors. The higher the value, the more reddish the color will be. You can check the skin weight value by entering the weight paint mode. More details will be covered later in this chapter.

Here's an example of how the skin weight looks like in Blender:

Now, what we need to do is properly name all the bones of the player character. You can do this by selecting each bone and changing its name in the Properties panel. You must give the same name for both the mirrored bones with a _L or _R behind the name, otherwise the mirror effect will be broken.

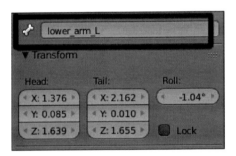

Next, select the mesh and go to the **Vertex Groups** section under the **Data** tab in the Properties panel. Create new vertex groups and give each of them the same name as the bones. Each of these vertex groups will act as a container to store the skin weight values in for each of the bones in the armature.

The name of the vertex groups needs to be exactly the same as the bones so that Blender knows which vertex group will be linked to which bone.

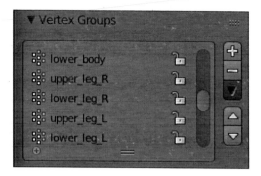

After this, batch-select the vertices that you want to be associated with a specific bone and assign them to the vertex group, which has the same name as the bone.

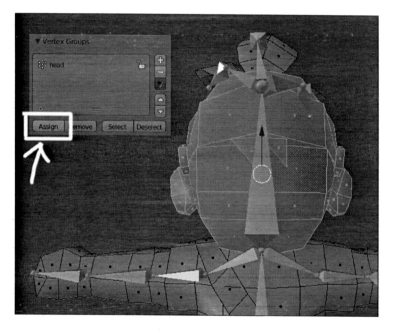

After you have assigned all the vertices to the bones, we can try to bind the armature to the mesh again. This time, however, instead of choosing automatic weights, we will pick the first option named **Armature Deform**. By choosing this option, Blender will help associate all the vertices in the vertex groups to the bones that it's named after and will simply assign the full skin weight (factor of 1.0) to these vertices. Don't worry about the values of the skin weights because we can adjust them later on.

If we don't adjust the skin weight, the mesh deformation will look really odd, and that makes the character look like a robot. To make the character look organic when animating, we need to adjust the values of the skin weights in the **Weight Paint** option. To enter the weight paint mode, select the mesh and click on **Weight Paint** in the combo box below the 3D view.

Weight painting

After you have entered the paint weight mode, you will see the whole character turn blue with a small section of red on its body. These colors represent the skin weight values of the vertices associated with a particular bone. You can try to select a different vertex group and see the colors changing. This is because you're now viewing the skin weight values associated with another bone.

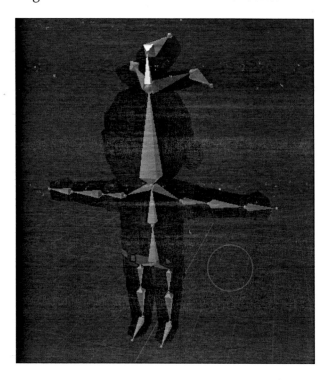

To change the value of the skin weights, we can *paint* the values using our mouse cursor. To change the size of the brush, go to the Tool Shelf and you will see the **radius** property under the **Brush** section. There are also some other options that you can set, such as the types of brushes, weight value, strength of the brush, blending mode, and so on and so forth.

There are also some advanced settings below it, but we will skip those for now.

To make the skin more fluid and less robotic when animating, make sure that each bone has some minor influence over the neighboring vertices beside the ones that are fully under its control. This will create slight stretches to the neighboring vertices when moving the bone, and this will create the illusion that the object is organic.

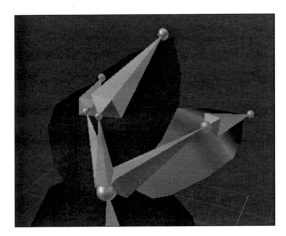

You may also note some visual artifacts when moving some of the bones. This happens because some of the vertices are not assigned to a vertex group due to carelessness. This problem can also be fixed by applying a full weight value to the vertices using the brush tool.

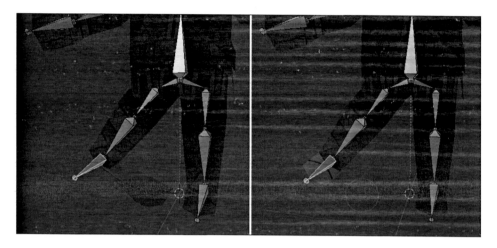

Play around with weight painting until there are no major problems occurring with your rig. Rigging and skinning are both very time consuming, but they're fun to work on once you're used to them!

Animating characters

Before we start animating our game characters, we need to set an important setting. Go to the **Render** tab in the Properties panel and find the **Frame Rate** option. Change the frame rate to 60 fps because that's what video games are running at. If you chose another option instead, your animation will seem like it is being played at a very slow speed in the game engine. So, make sure that this option is set before you start animating your character because prevention is better than cure.

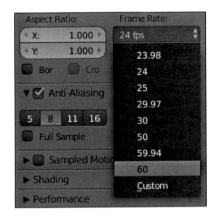

Game animation has adopted a technique from traditional animation named **key-framing**. Key-framing is the process of assigning a posture or specific parameter (such as position, rotation, and scale) to a character or object at a specific point in time. Each of these key-frames is then processed by the computer to generate the in-between frames through a process named **interpolation**. This eliminates the need to animate every single frame, which is a very tedious job.

There are several ways you can set key-frames to your bones. One of the methods is to tell Blender to automatically assign a new key-frame whenever you make some changes to a bone. This option can be activated by pressing the button with a red dot below the animation timeline. To deactivate it, press the button again.

However, I would not recommend you use automatic key-framing because despite its convenience, it often makes things worse by automatically recording all your mistakes as well. For example, you might want to do some testing on the rig but you've forgotten to turn off automatic key-framing. Once you've realized, you have already made tons of changes to the bones, which are now all being automatically recorded to the timeline. What could possibly go wrong?

To manually insert a key-frame, press *I* while the bone is still selected. A menu will pop up and ask you which parameter(s) need to be saved to the key-frame. This is very flexible as it allows you to save only those parameters that you need.

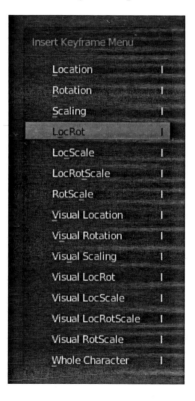

Always plan before you animate your character. I personally prefer to draw the poses on paper before touching Blender. This is because I can quickly draw out the poses on paper quickly and instantly decide whether it's a good posture or not, and then make changes without messing around with the software. "Oh, what's the shortcut key for rotation again?"

The advantage of having a proper plan for your animations is that you have already done all the brainstorming beforehand and once you're in Blender, you can straightaway lay down the key-frames quickly by following your sketches for every key-frame. This really speeds up the work; all you need to do now is make some minor adjustments and focus on the smaller details.

To adjust the key-frames, split your viewport and change the other half into the animation graph editor. The graph editor controls how key-frames are interpolated. You can adjust the animation curves, which represent parameters that are being interpolated from one key-frame to another. Alternatively, you can also use the NLA editor and dope sheet to adjust your key-frames.

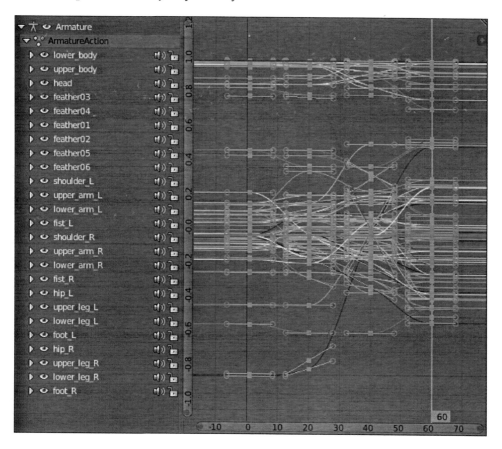

Regardless of which animation editor you're using, the controls are still identical to the 3D view: press *A* to select all or deselect all, press *B* for batch-select, *X* to delete key-frames, *G* to move key-frames, *R* to rotate, *S* for scale, and so on.

The 12 basic principles of animation

Animation is not something that can be mastered in a day or two. It takes tons of practice to become a good animator. However, if you learn the correct way to work on animations, such as by following a set of rules or principles, it will help you to achieve better results in a short amount of time.

The following are the 12 basic animation principles introduced by traditional hand-drawn animators from Disney back in the 1980's, which is now regarded as the *Bible of animation* by animators around the world.

1. **Squash and stretch**: Squash and stretch is a great way to exaggerate animations and add more appeals to the movement. It can be applied to everything, from a non-living object to a humanoid character. The best example of this is to look at a bouncing ball. As the ball starts to fall, it will stretch out just before impact, and as the ball impacts the ground, it squashes. Then, the ball stretches again as it takes off.

2. **Anticipation**: Anticipation is used in animation to get the audience ready for an action which is about to happen. For example, when a character is about to jump, it will squat down before making the jumping movement. This not only gets the momentum up, but also allows the audience to know this character is about to move.

3. **Staging**: Staging refers to the method used to set up the scene to keep the audience focused on the main subject and without getting distracted by other things. Although this principle is not relevant to in-game character animation, it will be really helpful when you work on the in-game cinematics.

4. **Straight ahead action and pose to pose**: Straight ahead and pose to pose refers to the two different techniques of animation. With straight ahead, you will create each pose of the animation one after another as you are going. With pose to pose, it's much more planned out; the most important poses are required to properly inform the actions that are added first to ensure that the posing and timing is correct before adding more details.

5. **Follow through and overlapping action**: Follow through is the idea that separate parts of the body will continue moving after the character has come to a stop. For example, a character may have stopped its footsteps, but the arms will continue to move for a while before settling. Overlapping action means different parts of the body will move at different time and speed, for example, movements in real life.

6. **Ease in and ease out**: Ease in and ease out is sometimes also referred to as slow in and slow out. As an object or character starts to move or goes to stop, there needs to be time for acceleration and deceleration to achieve a natural look.

7. **Arc**: In real life, almost everything moves in some kind of arcing motion, except robots. In order to achieve a natural and realistic movement, you should adhere to the principle of arcs when animating your game character.

8. **Secondary action**: Secondary action refers to creating actions that support the main action without taking away its attention.

9. **Timing and spacing**: Timing and spacing in animation is what gives objects and characters the illusion of moving within the laws of physics. The timing refers to the number of frames between two poses. Spacing, on the other hand, refers to how those individual frames are placed. If the spacing is close to the frames, the object moves slower; if the spacing is further apart the object moves faster.

10. **Exaggeration**: Exaggeration is used to push movements of a character further and create the illusion of the character's weight. Although exaggeration is mostly used to create extremely cartoony movements for stylized animation, it can also be used for realistic animation to make a movement more readable while staying true to reality.

11. **Solid drawing**: This principal only applies to 2D hand-drawn animation. A solid and accurate drawing is important in 2D animation in keeping the volume and weight of the characters consistent.

12. **Appeal**: Appeal is probably one of the most important things in animation. Your character design has to look charismatic and fit the character's personality. This holds true for both heroes and villains. Appeal also comes to the movement style of each of the character, which should reflect the uniqueness of that particular character so that it can stick out in the audience's (or player's, in this case) memory.

Even though some of the principles are not relevant to 3D in-game animation (such as staging and solid drawing), they might help you in the future when you work on 2D sprite animation or prerendered game cinematics.

Summary

In this chapter, you learned how to create simple rigs for our characters and how to animate them using Blender. We covered topics such as character rigging and how to create armature for both the monster and the player character. You also learned how to do weight-painting and how to animate the characters.

In the next chapter, we will learn how to create a beautiful game environment using Blender.

Creating the Environment

In this chapter, you will learn how to build the terrain and props for our game's environment. In this chapter, we will cover the following topics:

- Building terrain and wall models
- Building rock models
- Creating textures for terrain, wall, and rocks
- Building grass models
- Creating grass textures

Building terrain and wall models

We start building the environment by constructing the overall shape of the level, which consists of the terrain and the wall surrounding it, since this level is located in an underground setting. Always check back the environment concept art to make sure you don't leave out any of the important details.

Let's recall again how the environment concept art looks.

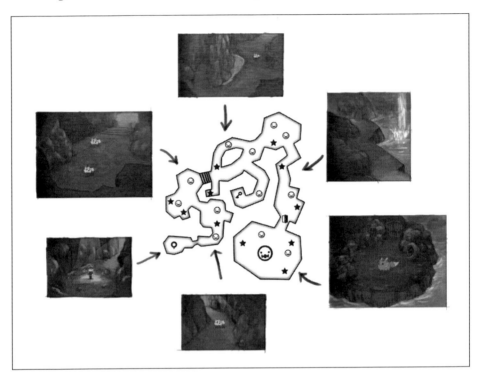

Even though Unity Engine has a built-in terrain editor, it's more suitable for an open world environment. In this case, however, we have to manually build the terrain from scratch in Blender and later import it to Unity.

In order to build the terrain accurately, we need to overlay the level layout design behind the 3D view in Blender so that we can follow it exactly when we build the terrain model. To do this, open up the 3D view's **Properties** panel by pressing *N*. Scroll down to the bottom and open up the section named **Background Images**. After this, click on **Add Image** and open the level layout design we did in *Chapter 1, Creating Your Game Concept*.

You probably won't see the layout appearing anywhere now because, by default, Blender uses the perspective view in the 3D viewport. In order to see the image, we have to switch from the perspective view to orthographic view by pressing the 5 key on your numpad. Then, press 7 on your numpad to switch to the top view so that we can construct the terrain by following the layout design.

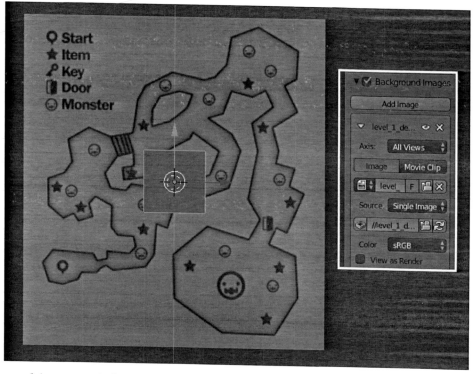

Numpad (or numeric keypad) allows you to navigate between different views in Blender. You can switch between the top view, front view, and side view by pressing 7, 1, and 3 respectively on your numpad. You can also switch between perspective and orthographic views using 5 on your nampad.

If you are using a laptop that has no numpad on it, you can ask Blender to reassign the keyboard numbers to act like the numpad buttons by going to **File** | **User Preferences** and clicking on the **Input** button on top. Then, on the left, you will see an option named **Emulate Numpad**. Tick the checkbox; you can now use the regular number buttons to switch between different views.

For more information, check out Blender's user manual here:
`http://www.blender.org/manual/getting_started/`
`basics/navigating/3d_view.html`

After you have switched to the orthographic top view, create a plane and start constructing the ground by using the various tools that we have learned in previous chapters. The best practice would be to move around the vertices using the grab tool and extrude the edges to fill in any empty spaces.

You don't have to worry about the height of the ground at this stage, just filling in the ground from a 2D point of view. You can refine the path and further adjust the width of the tunnels at this point. It's best to place the character model with the actual size on the ground and check whether the layout works as you imagined.

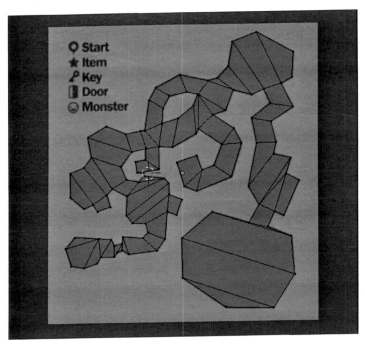

Then, select part of the ground vertices and move them slightly downwards. If you refer to the level concept, there are stairs somewhere in the level, which means that the latter part of the level is slightly lower in terms of terrain height.

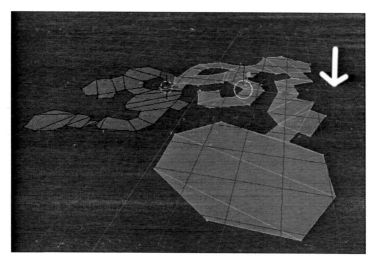

Next, create the tunnel's wall by selecting all the outer edges of the ground and extrude it upwards. You can hold the *Alt* key and right-click on the edges to batch-select the other edges that are connected to the one you're currently selecting. This speeds up the process a lot compared to manually selecting them edge by edge.

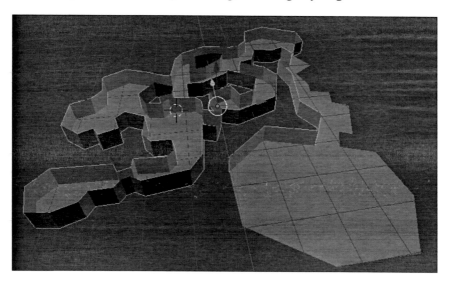

After this, extrude the wall outwards against the ground direction and connect it to the neighboring wall if there is one. Always check whether there are any hidden faces inside the mesh by switching over to the wireframe mode using the X key. Hidden faces may cause visual artifacts and should be fixed during the modeling stage.

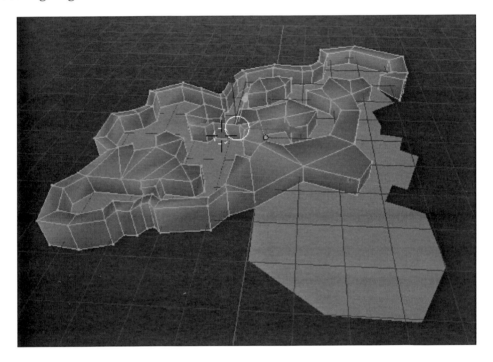

Finally, we will create cliffs by extruding the ground downwards. If you refer to the level concept, this area will be surrounded by water, which is why there is no wall around it.

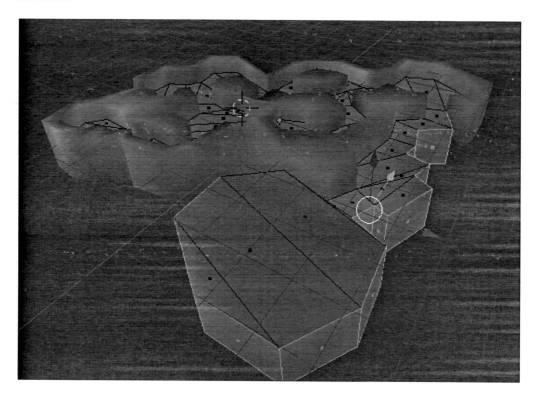

Building rock models

Next, we will construct rock models that will be used throughout the level. Props like this add variation to the level and hide texture seams on both the terrain and tunnel wall. We will get into this later on.

The easiest way to build a rock model is to start from a cube, and then slowly refine the shape using the loop-cut and knife tool. The knife tool is a handy tool in Blender that is used to split polygons into pieces. A user can initiate the knife tool by pressing *K*, and can define the cutting line by first clicking at the beginning of the line, followed by clicking on where you want the line to end.

In the following example, a cube is created using *Shift* + *A* and then going to **Mesh | Cube**. Then, enter Edit mode by pressing *Tab*, and then press *Ctrl* + *R* to initiate the Loop Cut tool. With this tool, cut the cube twice in two different directions and adjust the vertices manually to make it look more rounded. After this, use the knife tool by pressing *K* and cut out the top part into a shape of a rock.

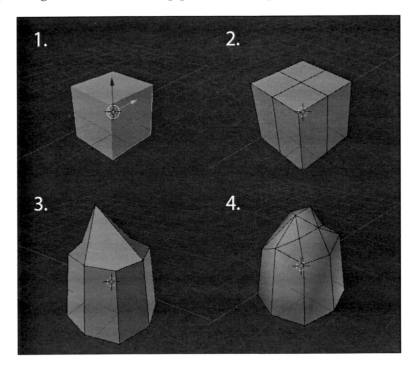

Do make sure that all the faces are either quads or triangles because any surfaces that consist of more than four vertices might cause a problem when the model is imported to the game engine. To avoid this problem, select all the faces and press *Ctrl + T* to triangulate all faces or press *Alt + J* if you want to convert them into quads instead of triangles.

Do note that most of the game engines, including the Unity Engine, which we're using in this book, prefer triangle faces instead of quad. However, when you export the mesh to the FBX format, the exporter will usually automatically convert the quads into triangles. This process does come with a risk because the exporter will decide on its own which direction the triangles should be when converting the faces, which might cause problems in parts of your model that will be deformed during animation, such as the elbow or the wrist. The best practice is to manually convert the faces of those critical parts into triangles while leaving the rest as quads. This way, your model will be easy to view in Blender, with less wireframe showing on screen, while keeping the topology correct for deformation.

Next, you can turn these rocks into larger boulder, by deleting the bottom surface and applying a mirror modifier to it. By using the preceding methods, you can easily create different types of rocks and make your level look more interesting.

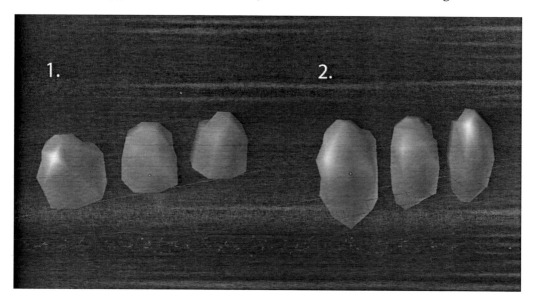

Creating rock and wall textures

Now we have created the models for the terrain, walls, and a bunch of rocks. However, without any textures, the players will not be able to tell what they actually resemble. Therefore, texturing is a very important step that helps to enhance the visual identity of a 3D object.

There are different ways to create a texture, depending on the art style you're after. For this game demo, I chose a semi-realistic environment art style, so I will be using photos to create all my environment textures. If you chose a cartoony style instead of realistic, you will need to manually paint your own texture. You can still make use of these photos but only as a reference for painting. Since the terrain, walls, and rocks belong to the same environment, logically, they all belong to the same type of mineral species. Therefore, we just need to create one single texture and reuse it for all the different 3D models. This not only makes the 3D assets look visually identical, but also increases your game's performance, which will be discussed in a later chapter.

In the following example, I used three different photos to create my final texture. Each of the photos contributes a very different level of detail to the final texture: an extremely rough surface with big cracks, a medium surface with decent bumpiness, and a fine surface with tiny poles. When you combine all of these different layers of detail into one, you will create a rather interesting looking texture, which is both rich in details but also harmonic to the eyes.

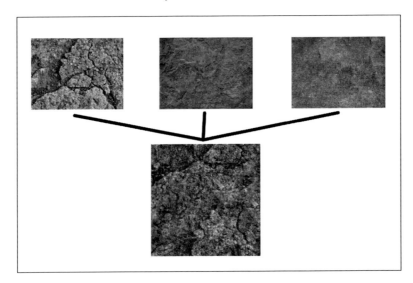

Then, I made the texture seamless so that it can be tiled on large models such as the terrain and walls. Different image editing software does this differently; if you're using Photoshop, go to **Filter | Other | Offset** to make your texture offset a certain amount of pixels. After this, use either the Healing Brush or Stamp Tool to remove the texture seam and you're almost done. Finally, since I'm going for a semi-realistic style, I have also adjusted the color of the texture and made it slightly more saturated to fit in with the cartoony characters.

Now I can apply the same textures to all the different rocks, and they will all look equally awesome!

For the terrain and walls, however, you will note that there are some repeating patterns when your camera is far away. Also, it looks super ugly and flat at this moment! Don't worry about this for now, though, as awesomeness will prevail after we add some lights and decals to the scene in a later chapter. Be patient. For now, it's all good.

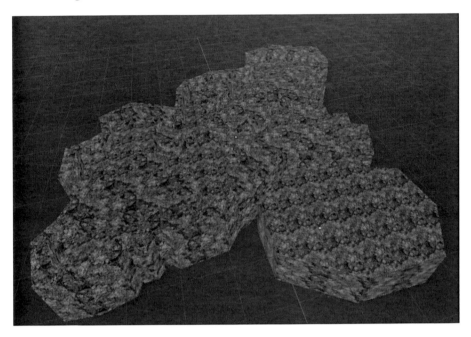

Building grass models

When I was designing the level concept for this game demo, I thought it would be better to have something to break the singularity of having only one type of hue in the level due to the fact that in an underground setting, there aren't many props that we can place to the level beside rocks. Well, we can place crystals all over the level, which will emit different colors of light, but that sounds like a lazy solution to me; besides, aren't most other games out there doing the same thing? I thought we could go for something different, so instead of shiny crystals, I decided to place a bunch of grass around the level instead.

First of all, grass can still grow underground provided that there are holes on the ceiling that allow the sunlight to enter underground. Second, this allows us to play around with the lighting to make the underground level look more interesting, and finally, by combining a green color with brown, we achieved color harmonic for this level, and that will definitely enhance the visual quality of this game due to the fact that these two colors are complementary colors on the color wheel. Complementary colors are any two colors that are directly opposite each other, such as red and green, red and purple, as well as yellow and green. When a pair of opposite colors is placed next to each other, it creates some striking optical effects whereby both colors cancel each other out, resulting in what we called **color harmonic**.

 For more information regarding complementary colors and color harmonies, search for basic color theory on a search engine.

The process of building a grass model is actually much easier than you would have imagined. Until this day, game developers around the world, including the AAA studios, are still using this same old technique to create the illusion of living grass in their games—using a bunch of planes and intersecting them in random directions. This technique is not perfect, of course, but so far, it's the best method, which is well-balanced between visual quality and performance.

To create a grass model in Blender, start with a plane, scale it slightly using the *S* key, and then duplicate the plane several times using *Shift + D* and rotate all the planes using the *R* key to cover all different directions. You can slowly adjust the planes' rotation again after applying texture to the model because it's easier to examine the result with texture on it.

Before we're done with the grass model, combine all the planes into a single object by selecting all the planes and then pressing *Ctrl + J*. Then, duplicate the grass model and flip the normals of the duplicated mesh by entering Edit mode, and then select all the faces and go to **Mesh | Normals | Flip Normals** from the 3D View Menu.

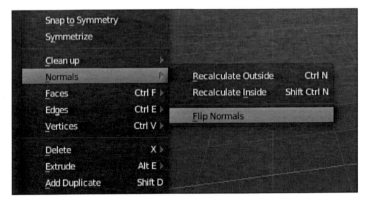

The reason we do this is because in the game engine, only one side of the polygon will be rendered, unlike in Blender where both sides will be rendered. To address this issue, we have duplicated the entire mesh and flipped the normals of the duplicated mesh so that the other side of the polygon is also being rendered when the model is imported to the game engine.

Creating the grass texture

Next, we will create the texture for our grass. This is also a lot easier than you might have thought. First of all, using your choice of image editing software, draw out the shape of a clump using just plain color. You can use any tools you like, such as the paint tool, lasso tool, pen tool, and so on. It also doesn't need to be extremely accurate because we're going for a semi-realistic style. After you are done with the shape, apply a gradient color to it: darker green at the bottom and lighter green on top. Next, overlay a leaf texture on top of it to add some subtle details to the texture.

Then, you're done!

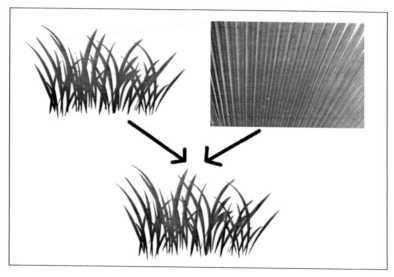

You can now apply the texture to the grass model and adjust the planes again until you're satisfied. Do refer to *Chapter 2, Creating Characters,* if you have forgotten how to apply the texture to your model.

Summary

In this chapter, you learned how to create interesting looking environment models and props based on the initial-level concept design. We discussed how to construct an entire terrain in Blender and how to create different types of props with beautiful textures to enhance the visual quality of the game environment.

In the next chapter, you will learn how to import all the assets that we created in Blender into Unity Game Engine and start creating the actual game!

5
Integrating Your Assets into the Game

In this chapter, we will learn how to use software named Unity, which is used to develop games. We will learn how to import the 3D models that we built in Blender, as well as the textures that we created earlier into Unity. After this, we will put everything together to form a level.

In this chapter, we will cover the following:

- Basic user interface of Unity
- Import environment assets
- Introducing prefabs
- Setting up terrain
- Setting up water surfaces
- Setting up foliage
- Setting up environment lighting
- Optimizing scenes with occlusion culling
- Importing character assets

Basic user interface of Unity

First of all, let's take a look at its user interface. Unity's user interface is much simpler when compared with Blender because Blender is complex software that allows you to do so many things, including modeling, texturing, sculpting, rigging, animation, tracking, and compositing. However, Unity is software that focuses only on game-related functionality. Therefore, you can't edit the 3D models in Unity but instead have to import them from 3D modeling software like Blender.

Without wasting much time, let's take a look at Unity's user interface, as shown here:

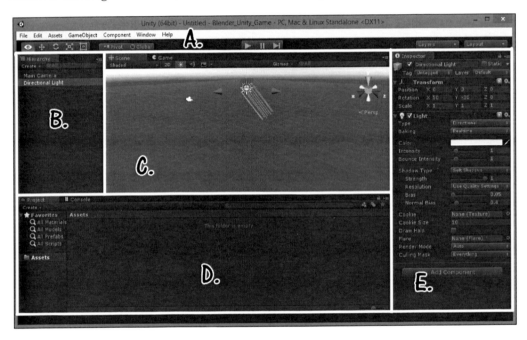

- **Toolbars (A)**: Here lies the application menu toolbar as well as a simple navigation toolbar located below it. There are three special buttons located in the middle of the navigation toolbar, which are unique to Unity. When the play button is pressed, you will instantly enter to the game mode and will start testing your game. To exit from the game mode, simply press the stop button. This allows you to quickly test your game repeatedly and iterate the game variables to make sure that your game is balanced.

- **Hierarchy (B)**: This is where all the objects in the scene are listed. The list also shows the parent-child relationship between objects, and it allows you to change the relationship by simply selecting the object from the list and dragging it to another object.

- **Scene View and Game View (C)**: The **Scene** panel is where you edit your game scene, and the Game panel is where you test your game. When the play button is pressed, Unity will automatically switch over to the game panel and then back to the scene panel again when you pressed the stop button.

- **Project Browser (D)**: The Project Browser displays all the assets in your project. This panel splits into two sides: on the left, we have the directory hierarchy and when you click on one of the folders, the assets contained in the selected folder will be shown to the right of the panel.

- **Inspector (E)**: When an object from the scene is selected, the object's components and properties will be shown in this **Inspector** panel. You can add/remove components or change its properties on this panel.

Unity provides more panels/windows than what we have just introduced. However, the other panels are being hidden by default. You can unhide them by going to the menu toolbar and choose **Windows** and select the panel you want to unhide. By default, when you open up a new panel, it will appear as an individual window. You can join the window with other existing panels by clicking on the window's **Header** tab and dragging it to the side of the other panels that you want it to join together with. Then, release your mouse and see the window disappear and turn into a panel instead, being located side by side with the other panels. Unity's user interface is very flexible and able to fit to your preferences.

Importing environment assets

After learning about Unity's user interface, let's import all the assets we did in the previous chapters into our Unity project! There are several ways in which you can import your assets. The first way is to copy the files into the `Assets` folder in your project directory. Unity will detect the files and convert them to its native format automatically.

Don't worry as Unity practices non-destructive approaches, which means it doesn't actually do anything to your original files. Instead, it places the converted files into temporary folders within the project directory, which are hidden away from the engine users.

The second method is to drag the source files directly to the **Project** panel in Unity. Your files will be copied to the Assets folder and get converted to the native format automatically. After this, you will be able to see thumbnails of your assets showing up on the Project Browser. You will also see an additional folder being created named Materials. This will happen when you import any 3D models to your game project. The folder contains materials that are having the same name and basic properties (usually color and texture) as the 3D models that you just imported. It saves your time for having to create the materials one by one from scratch.

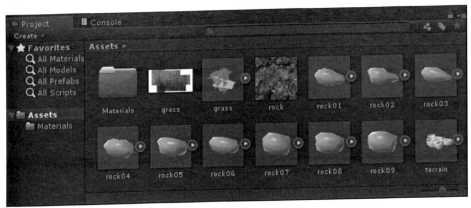

The first thing I always do after importing all the assets to my game project is to tidy up the directory. I categorize the assets and place them into different subfolders, such as Meshes, Textures, and so on. It's always a good thing to start arranging your assets properly early on. As your project progresses, there will be more and more assets being added to your project, and it will be much harder to tidy up your project directory by then.

Before we start placing the meshes to the scene, one important step that we need to do is to ensure that the import settings have been set correctly. Select one of the meshes in the Project Browser and you will see the import settings appearing on the **Inspector** panel. The import settings can be set differently depending on how you use the mesh in your game: whether your mesh has blend shapes or colliders, or require an extra UV map for light map baking, and so on. It really depends on your game's requirement.

In this case, I need all my rocks and terrain to have collision, as well as a UV map to generate light map; therefore, I enable those options in the import settings.

I have also enabled **Optimize Mesh** and set the **Mesh Compression** setting to **Medium** so that Unity helps to automatically optimize the meshes without any manual labor work. These options, however, might cause visual artifacts to the meshes, so you really have to check it multiple times to avoid such problems. Try to lower down the **Mesh Compression** setting if it causes visual artifacts to your mesh. I applied the same settings to all the rock meshes as well as the terrain. For the grass model, I disabled **Generate Colliders** because we don't want our characters to collide and get stuck within the bushes. Instead, we want them to be able to move through the grass without any obstruction.

After this, start placing each of the meshes to the scene by dragging them from the Project Browser to the Scene View. Alternatively, you can also drag the meshes to the **Hierarchy** panel, both ways work the same. The reason we do this is to set up the meshes properly. Later on, we will turn them into what we call prefabs.

Introducing prefabs

Prefabs are basically templates from which you can create new object instances in the scene. We only need to set up the asset once – the material, texture, physics settings, and so on – and pack them into prefabs. After this, we only need to place the prefabs around the scene without repeating the same steps (setting up the material, texture, physics settings, and so on) again and again for each identical asset. When we change the properties of a prefab (for example, changing the texture), the same properties in all the instances linked to this particular prefab will also be changed.

Prefab is something really important, that often saves us from lots of trouble and hassle. For example, say you have finally placed all the 300 palm tree meshes to your game scene without using any prefab. Then, all of a sudden, your art director realized that the size of the trees is very big and should be scaled down by 20%. Without using any prefab, the only way to do this is to scale all the tree meshes one by one. Likewise, you will only need to set the correct scale in the source prefab, and all the tree instances in the scene will be changed instantly. Work smart!

Setting up the terrain

At this stage, place only the terrain and rock meshes to the scene because they all share the same texture and material. Then, create a new material and rename it to rock. Click on the small rectangle icon in front of the **Albedo** property and select the rock texture.

Now, apply this material to the meshes in the scene by dragging the material from the Project Browser directly to the specific object in the scene.

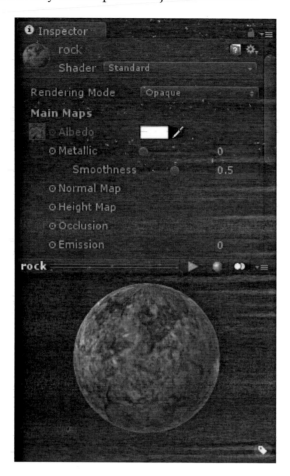

Now that we have placed the terrain and all rocks to the scene and applied the material to all of them, it's time to pack them into prefabs! It's extremely easy to achieve this. All you need to do is drag the game object from the **Hierarchy** panel back to the Project Browser. When you change the properties of a prefab instance in the scene, the properties of the other instances will not be changed. However, if you click on the **Apply** button on the **Inspector** panel, it will then apply the changes to the source prefab, which subsequently changes all the other prefab instances as well.

After this, place the rock prefabs around the scene to make it look more interesting! The terrain, especially the wall, looks really smooth now, so we need to place some rocks on the wall to make the surface uneven and look more *rockier*. You can do this in Blender as well, but it's very hard to change it later on, and furthermore, the polygon count will be extremely high because each rock is a totally distinct individual mesh with a set of polygon data.

If you do this in Unity, however, each rock is just an instance of an existing prefab, which shares the polygon data across the entire map; this saves a lot of resources and gain better performance for your game. Besides, since the prefab instances are not combined together as a huge chunk of mesh unlike what happens if you do it in Blender, it can also take advantage of the occlusion culling feature in Unity, which hides any game object, that is not within the eyesight of the game camera. We will discuss more about this later.

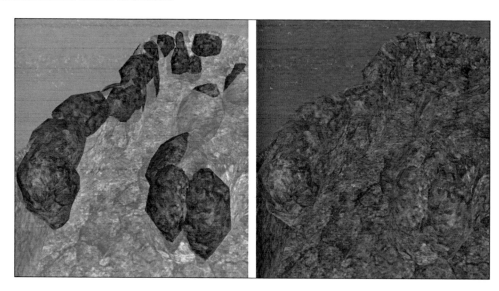

Setting up water surfaces

After you have done placing all the rock prefabs around the scene, we will now proceed to something simpler, but interesting—water surfaces. If you refer back to the environment concept, there are basically two areas that have water containment: one is the small area within the terrain and another one is a big volume of water surrounding the terrain.

Normally in video games, water surfaces are planes with fancy material applied on it to make it look like water. It's the same in our case; let's create a plane by going to **Game Object | 3D Object | Plane**. Select the plane by using the left mouse button and press *W* to enable transform manipulator. Move the plane to the location you want and scale the plane by switching over to scale manipulator using the *R* key in order to fill the entire pit with the water. It is okay to intersect the plane with the terrain as the player will not be able to see what's underneath the terrain.

Then, create a new material and apply a texture to the **Albedo** property. I grabbed a free seamless water texture from the Internet, which looks really nice and fits my purpose. In my case, my water texture looks too whitish, so I adjusted the color of the albedo to bright ocean blue. I also adjusted the metallic and smoothness values to give the water surface a little bit of specularity. Do note that if you set the alpha value of the color lower, your water doesn't actually become more transparent. This is because the rendering mode of your material is currently set to **Opaque**. You need to set it to the **Transparent** mode to make use of the alpha value. Depending on the size of your water surface, you might also want to change the tiling value of your texture so that the scale of your texture matches your visual goal.

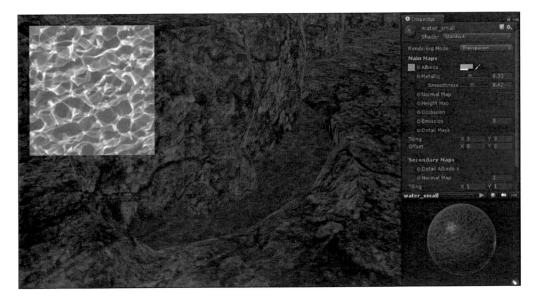

Next, create another plane. This time, scale it into a massive gigantic plane and place it somewhere below the ground level. Duplicate the previous material by selecting the material in the project panel and press *Ctrl + D*. Rename the material and set the texture tilling to an even higher value to match the size of the plane. Your level should look something like this by now.

Setting up foliage

Currently, our cave looks really boring with just rocky surfaces everywhere, so let's pull in the grass model and the decal texture that we did in the previous chapter! For the decal, the method is similar to what we did to the water surface — create a plane, a material with the decal texture applied to its albedo property, and apply the material to the plane you just created. Then, set the rendering mode to **Fade** and you'll get a nice-looking decal with smooth transparency around the texture. The transparent mode is not suitable in this case, as it will create a white halo around the transparent area, which is not the correct visual that we're looking for. After this, pull the game object back to the Project Browser to pack it into a prefab.

Next, place the grass model into the scene, create a new material for it, and apply the grass texture to the Albedo property. For the grass material, set the rendering mode to **Cutout** instead of any other modes. If you set the rendering mode to **Fade** or **Transparent**, the polygon sorting will not be correct, and hence there will be an odd-looking visual artifact created. After this, drag the grass object to the Project Browser to pack it into a prefab.

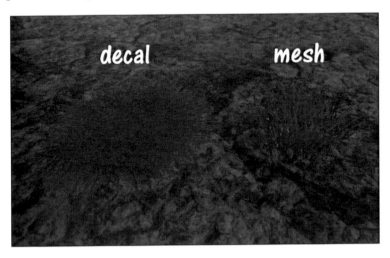

The reason we created the decal is to use it as a *carpet* below the grass models. Without the decal, the grass will look as if it suddenly pops out from the rock and won't look as convincing to viewers. Instead, if we place the grass models on top of the decals, it will look more natural and make more sense.

Setting up environment lighting

After you have placed the grass around, it's time to set up the lighting. There are several types of lighting, including ambient light, spot light, directional light, point light, and so on. Each type of light serves a different purpose and produces different effect, so you have to be really sure what kind of outcome you're looking for before deciding the type of light to use.

The first thing you need to do is delete all the existing lights in the scene. It's better to start from complete dark and slowly add in different light sources one by one. Next, go to **Window | Lighting** and open up a new **Lighting** panel. Change **Ambient Source** to **Gradient** and set the three colors below it to something bluish, gradually becoming darker. This will set the overall ambient mood for our scene.

Since our scene is supposedly located in a dungeon, we shouldn't be seeing the sky at all. So, I went back to Blender and created a huge cave wall surrounding the terrain. This can be easily achieved by creating a sphere; squash it a little and adjust some of the vertices to add some irregularity to its appearance. Then, select all the faces and flip the normal's direction by going to the Tool Shelf and clicking on **Shading/UVs** tab, click on the **Flip Direction** option under **Normals**. Export the cave from Blender to Unity and viola! If the texture scale seems to be off, you can either change the texture tilling settings in the material or adjust the UV scale of the cave wall in Blender.

Viola! The scene now looks more like a dungeon.

Next, we will start adding actual light sources to the scene. If you haven't already deleted all the lights in the scene, especially the default sun light (directional light), do it now. Since our scene is located in a dungeon, no sun light is able to reach here, and it's not logical to use directional light in this case. Besides this, I always turn off the **Continuous Baking** setting on the **Lighting** panel because I prefer to manually bake the lighting.

Create a point light by going to **Game Object | Light | Point Light**. Adjust the range and intensity to something that you think matches your visual goal and then place more lights to the entire scene by duplicating the first point light.

Use the light sources to guide the player around the level, because players tend to subconsciously follow the path that has brighter light on the other end and won't go for the dark.

Once the lighting has been set up, select all the meshes in the scene and tick the **Static** option on the **Inspector** panel. This step is crucial because the light map will only be generated for the static meshes. Then, go to **Lighting** panel and click on the **Build** button. If the lightmap is not baked correctly, check your mesh settings again. Select the meshes in the Project Browser and make sure that the **Generate lightmap UV into UV2** option is enabled.

A light map is essentially a texture that stores the brightness of the surface of a 3D model the later use. The brightness is precalculated by the game engine based on the surrounding lighting set up by the level designer. The light map allows the game to display sophisticated lighting effects, such as Global Illumination, at a relatively low computational cost.

If everything goes flawlessly, you should be able to get a nicely lit dungeon that gives players the sense of danger—mysterious and adventurous!

Optimizing the scene with Occlusion Culling

Next, we will optimize the scene by using a method named **Occlusion Culling**. This technique generates partitions in the 3D space and assigns each game object into the partition that occupies the same space with the object. During the game mode, Unity will hide all the game objects that are not being seen by the in-game camera by checking which partition is within the camera view frustum and which partition is not.

Open up the **Occlusion** panel by going to **Window | Occlusion Culling**. Click on the **Bake** button to generate the partitions for the first time to check whether the size is correct. Each partition (or occluder) should not be too huge as it will decrease the effectiveness of the culling process. Set the **Smallest Occluder** setting to adjust the size of the partitions. The screenshot that illustrates the different outcome by putting a different value to the **Smallest Occluder** setting is as follows. After the baking process is complete, you can check the result by selecting the camera and choose **Visualize** option in the drop-down menu located in the small **Occlusion Culling** window appearing in your scene panel. Do note that the more complex your scene is, the longer it will take to bake the light maps.

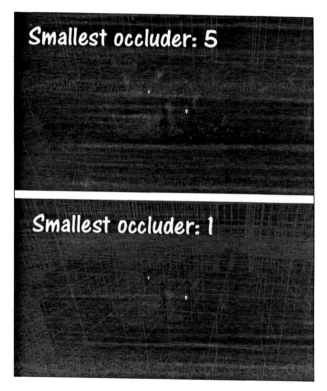

Importing character assets

We have just completed our level's environment. Now, let's import the characters! The process is similar to importing the environment assets — drag the models to the scene, apply a material to it, and we're almost done. One of the most important aspects that makes the characters feel alive is animation. Without any animation, your characters will just look like props and not living things. In previous chapters, you have already learned how to animate the characters in Blender and how to export the animations alongside the 3D models. Even though we are not using the animations in this chapter yet, we need the right settings so that the animations are ready to be used at anytime in the following chapters.

To set up animations for the characters, we need to go back to the Project Browser and select the character's mesh. In the **Inspector** panel, click on the **Animations** button to open up the animation settings interface. Under the **Clips** section, you can add or remove animations by clicking on the **+** and **−** buttons. To edit each of the animations, select the animation from the list and all the properties of the animation will be shown below the list. You can change the name, start frame, end frame as well as other properties. You can also preview the animation at the bottom part of the panel. Once you're done, click on the **Apply** button and you're good to go!

Next, you will learn how to call these animations during gameplay. Even though we have set the animations, such as idle, run, and attack, the animations are not linked to your character prefab just yet. In order to do so, you need to create something named **Animator Controller** in Unity, which is part of the animation system in Unity named **Mechanim**. An Animator Controller allows you to arrange and maintain a set of animations for a character or an object and manages the various animation states and transitions between them using a flow chart system named **state machine**.

An Animation controller exists as an asset in Unity, so in order to create one, you can go to **Assets | Create | Animator Controller**, or just right-click on the Project Browser and then go to **Create | Animator Controller** to create one. To edit the controller, double-click on the file you just created, and Unity will automatically open up an **Animator** window.

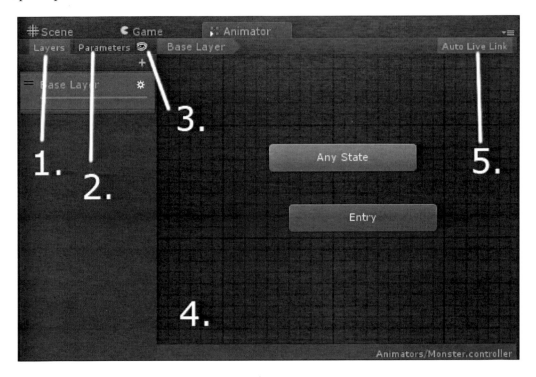

Let's take a closer look at the **Animator** window:

- **Layers**: This allows you to manage complex state machines for different body parts. For example, if you have a character who walks around while shooting, you can create two different animation layers: one for the upper body and another for the lower body, with each control different state machines of different body part, allowing both running and shooting animations to coexist within the same character mesh.

- **Parameters**: This contains the variables that are defined within an animator controller that can be accessed and assigned values from scripts. This is how you can control or affect the flow of the state machine through scripting.

- **Show/Hide side panel**: You can show or hide the side panel on the animator window by pressing this button.

- **Node Editor**: This is the main layout of the **Animator** window where you would edit the flow of the animation states. Each state is represented by a rectangular block, which we refer as a node. Every node can be linked to each other for state transition. Above the **Editor** panel, you can see another panel with the word **Base Layer.** This is the hierarchical breadcrumb where you can jump back and forth to the substates of a node or to the parent states of the current state.

- **Auto Live Link**: When **Auto Live Link** is enabled, Unity will display an animation with a highlight on the **Animator** window to show which state is being played during gameplay.

By default, you will see two bars within the **Animator** window: **Any State** and **Entry**. Each of these bars is called an **animation state,** and they can be navigated to one another based on the conditions you set and the way you link the states together. The **Entry** state is where the state machine starts from. The state that it points to will be the default animation state of the controller. On the other hand, the **Any State** state allows you to make a transition from any one of the animation states to the state it's pointing to.

Now it's time to add the animations that we have set up previously to the animator controller. It's very easy to get this done, all you need to do is click on the little arrow icon besides the character mesh to expand it and search for the animation clips, which you created previously by setting the start frame and end frame. Click and drag the animation clip directly to the animator window and you will see a new animation state being added to the animator window with the name matching the clip you just dragged.

The first animation clip being added to the animator window will be linked to the entry state and change its color from gray to orange, which indicates that it is the default state. Alternatively, you can also drag the mesh to the **Animator** window without expanding it, and that will directly add all the animation clips contained within the mesh.

Next, we will make a transition from the **Idle** state to the **Running state** by right-clicking on the **Idle** state and select **Make Transition** from the pop-up menu. A line with an arrow in the middle will appear and follow your cursor around, which indicates that the animation state is now ready to link to the other state. Move your cursor to the animation state, which you want it to navigate to, in this case, the **Running** state, and left-click on it. The line will now connect from the **Idle** state to the **Running** state; this indicates that the **Running** state can be navigated from the **Idle** state if the conditions meet, which we will discuss later. Now, let's right-click on the **Running** state, select **Make Transition** and click on the **Idle** state to make a transition back to the **Idle** state.

This is important because we want to return to idling animation when the character is not running around.

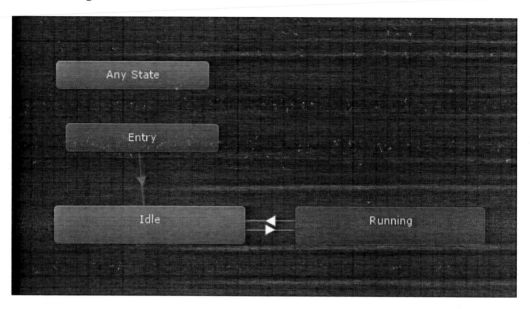

After this, we need to create a parameter in order to be used as a condition for the animation states to change. The condition to change from idling to running, and vice versa, is obviously the movement speed of the player. Therefore, we need to create a floating point number as a parameter for the condition. To do this, go to the Parameter tab on the side panel of **Animation** window, click on the **+** button, and select **Float** from the pop-out menu. A new parameter will then be added to the **Parameters** tab. Rename the parameter to `runningSpeed` and lead the default value as `0.0`.

Now that you have created the parameter, we can use it as the condition to navigate between states. Click on one of the arrows connecting the **Idle** state and **Running** state, the **Inspector** window will now display the properties of that particular transition. Scroll down to the bottom of the **Inspector** window and you will see a section named **Condition**. Click on the **+** button below it to add a new condition and then select the parameter you want from the drop-down box. If you only have one parameter, it will be selected automatically by default. You will see another drop-down box besides the parameter name with two options: **Greater** and **Less**, and a text field besides it. These three options form a condition that allows a state to transition to another state when the requirement is met.

For example, if we want to navigate from the **Idle** state to the **Running** state, the
runningSpeed should be higher than zero because the player will start moving.
Therefore, the condition for the transition should be:

runningSpeed	Greater	0

On the other hand, if we want the animation to return to **Idle** state when player stops
moving, the condition will look like so:

runningSpeed	Less	1

The number behind varies between different projects due to different scaling factor,
so make sure that you check what number is best suited for you.

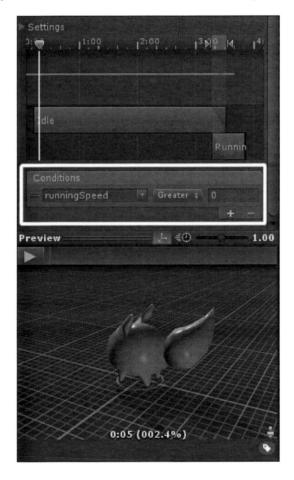

You can create several other conditions for different animations, such as jump, attack, damage, death, and so on. Usually, animations that are related to movements (running, jumping, and so on) use float or integer parameter type for its condition, whereas other types of animations that get played by triggering (attack, damage, death, and so on) usually use Boolean or trigger parameter type for its condition. You can learn more about animation parameters from the Unity Manual at `http://docs.unity3d.com/Manual/AnimationParameters.html`.

Once you have linked all the animation states together, the animator controller is now ready to be used by the character prefab! Select your character prefab and look for the **Animator** component. By default, the **Controller** option is empty. Drag the animator controller you created previously from the Project Browser directly to the **Controller** option on the **Inspector** window. Then, click on the **Apply** button at the top of the **Inspector** window to save your character prefab and it's now ready to be used! You will learn how you can change the parameters of the animation controllers and make it navigate between different animation states in the next chapter because it has to be done via scripting.

Summary

In this chapter, you learned how to import environment assets and pack them into reusable templates named prefabs. You have also learned how to form a game level by putting all the assets together and rearrange them accordingly. Besides, you also learned how to set up lighting and optimize the scene so that your game can be run in the best performance. Last but not least, you also learned how to set up the characters including their animations.

In the next chapter, we will discuss how to develop the game structure, implement the gameplay, and start writing some serious code!

6
Developing the Game Structure

In this chapter, we will learn what game structure is and how we design our game structure using flow charts, and implement it in our game in Unity using C language.

In this chapter, we will cover:

- Introduction to game structure design
- Planning the game flow
- Designing the user interface structure
- Player inputs and character movements
- Creating basic artificial intelligence

Introduction to game structure design

Video games have evolved over the past decades to become more and more sophisticated in both their storytelling techniques and gameplay mechanics. This, in turn, has made the game development process even more complicated as game programmers are no longer the ones who also design the game mechanics or the ones who decide the storyline.

Therefore, game developers had to find a way to streamline the development workflow so that both the designers and programmers could communicate more closely to make sure that there is no conflict between the game design and technical implementation during the production stage. This resulted in an emphasis on the importance of game structure design during the pre-production stage. From the game structure, developers will be able to see the bigger picture and point out possible improvements for the game before they start implementing it.

Game structure consists of several different categories, including the flow of the user interface, finite state machine, game mechanics design, decision-making chart for AI, and so on. Before we even start writing any game code, we should first of all plan the flow of our game: how the game should behave, starting from the moment it's launched; what should happen next; whether to display a cinematic before proceeding to the main menu; what the enemies do when they have detected the presence of the player, and so on. From there, we break down the structures into different subcategories and start designing it using a flow chart.

There are plenty of free tools out there that can be used to draw the flow charts, such as OpenOffice, LibreOffice, draw.io, Gliffy, and so on. Pick the tool that is most suited to you.

Planning the game flow

Let's start creating our game structure by planning the game flow. Game flow is the overall flow of our game, from the moment it's launched to finally quitting the game. From the game flow, we will be able to see the big picture of how our game is going to work.

For example, a typical game flow may look like this:

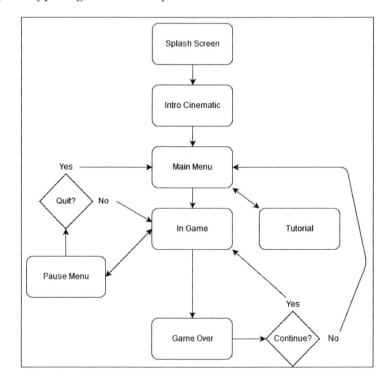

A flow chart like this usually starts from the top going downwards. You can also put an indication for the starting node such as a different background color, apply bold text, or put an icon beside the text. After that, arrows will be used to indicate how the game state is being navigated based on given conditions. Diamond shapes will be used when there is more than one condition, and each of them will yield a different result, hence its arrow will be pointing to a different state. Two-way arrows will be used for two-way navigation between two states.

By looking at the preceding chart, we are able to tell that the game contains an introduction cinematic right after the splash screen, as well as a tutorial level that can be entered from the main menu. The flow chart is self-explanatory and requires no extra explanation for the developers to understand the flow of the game, and this automatically makes the communication between different departments easier.

By looking at the flow chart, game programmers are able to list the features that are required for the game (for example, a full-screen video player is required in order to play the intro cinematic) and start working on them. At this point, however, we shouldn't dive into the details, such as how the main menu works, what the tutorial should look like, and so on. We should first get the overall picture right before going into details. This way, we can avoid design problems that may occur during the production stage. For our game, however, it is much simpler. We do not have any introduction cinematic, game options, as well as a tutorial level, so we will just keep those three out from our chart.

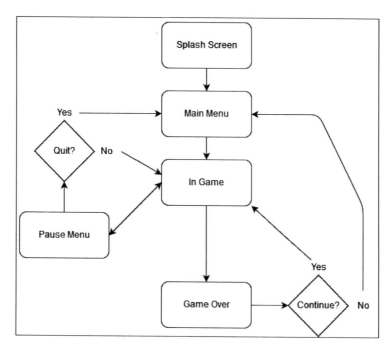

Now that we have the flow chart ready, you can send it to your team members and get them to implement the game flow. If you are the sole developer, however, I will teach you how to implement the flow chart into your game! Since the splash screen is the first state in the flow chart, and also probably the easiest one to make, we will learn how to create our game's splash screen in Unity.

First, open up your Unity project from the previous chapter. Then, create a new scene and name it SplashScreen. The naming is important because we will be using it for jumping from one scene to another later in this chapter. After that, we will see an empty scene that has a sky box applied by default. We don't want that for our splash screen, so we will create a 2D background to hide the sky box from the player.

To do that, we need to first of all create a canvas that acts like a container for our user interface objects. Go to **Game Object | UI | Canvas** to create the canvas. After that, create an image object by selecting the canvas and going to **Game Object | UI | Image**. A white rectangle will be created on the screen, but it does not cover the entire screen. To solve that issue, select the image object and open up the **Inspector** panel. In the **Inspector** panel, you will see a box icon under **Rect Transform**. Click on that icon to open up the **Anchor Presets** window.

Select the icon in the bottom-right corner, which will make the image stretch along both axes. After that, make sure "Left", "Top", "Right", and "Bottom" are all set to 0. Now, the white image will cover the entire screen, which covers the 3D scene entirely.

Next, create another image object and apply your team's logo to it. Make sure the texture type of the image is set to "Sprite (2D and UI)", otherwise it cannot be used in the image object.

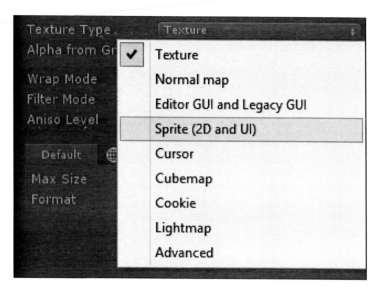

Once you're done, you will get this result:

But we don't want a static splash screen like this as it's kind of boring. Let's learn how to create a splash screen that fades in slowly before jumping over to the main menu. To achieve this, you'll need some scripting.

Create a new C# script in Unity by going to **Assets** | **Create** | **C# Script**. Name the script as `SplashScreen.cs` and double-click on it to open it up with the default script editor, that installed together with Unity, called MonoDevelop. By default, the newly created script is not empty. Unity has already written the class for you, which is named after your script's filename.

Inside the class, there are two functions: one called `Start()` and another called `Update()`. Both of these functions are built-in functions of Unity, which will be automatically called by Unity when the game is running. The `Start()` function only runs once when the scene has started (or when an object has spawned), as the function name implies. The `Update()` function, however, gets called by Unity in every game loop (or every tick). If your game is running at 60 frames per second, the `Update()` function will be called 60 times in a second.

Before you start writing any code, let's add this dependency called `UnityEngine.UI` to the top of your script. This is required for later use.

```
using UnityEngine.UI;
```

After that, within the `SplashScreen` class, we will add three variables: the first is the pointer to the logo object, the second variable is the color of the logo for us to change the opacity later, and the third is the speed of the opacity change. I added `public` in front of `Image` and `lerp` multiplier variables so that the variables will later appear on Unity's **Inspector** panel for us to link the logo object to this script.

```
public Image logo;
Color logoColor;
public lerpMultiplier = 0.02f;
```

Next, we will tell Unity what to do when the scene is first loaded, by writing code within the `Start()` function. We declare the `logoColor` variable in the form of RGBA and set it to transparent. Then, we make our logo transparent by applying `logoColor` to its `color` variable. After that, we execute `GotoMainMenu()` by using the `StartCoroutine()` function, which we will declare later.

```
void Start ()
{
   logoColor = new Color (1, 1, 1, 0);
   logo.color = logoColor;

   StartCoroutine (GotoMainMenu());
}
```

A **coroutine** is a special function that can stretch out over many ticks without stopping the rest of the game from going forward.

GotoMainMenu is a custom function that we wrote ourselves, which means Unity will not bother about it until we execute the function ourselves. In the GotoMainMenu() function, we ask the function to delay for 4 seconds before executing the next line of the function, which loads the main menu scene.

```
IEnumerator GotoMainMenu()
{
    yield return new WaitForSeconds(4);
    Application.LoadLevel ("MainMenu");
}
```

After that, we will write the code that makes the logo fade in over time. To achieve this, we need to write the code inside the Update() function, because the Update() function gets called on every tick; therefore, it can alter the transparency value over time.

We use a function from the Color class called Lerp(), which does exactly this— changing a color variable to a target color over a period of time. The Lerp() function requires three input variables: the first one is the original color, which is the color of the logo; the second variable is the target color; and the last variable is the speed at which the color changes over time. After that, we apply the color again to the logo.

```
void Update ()
{
    logoColor = Color.Lerp(logoColor, new Color(1, 1, 1, 1),
    Time.time * lerpMultiplier);
    logo.color = logoColor;
}
```

There you have it; we have completed the splash screen. However, don't forget to apply the `SplashScreen` script to an object in the scene; in this case, I applied the script to the camera, and then dragged the logo object to the `logo` variable of the script in the **Inspector** panel.

This is an overview of the full script:

```
using UnityEngine;
using System.Collections;

using UnityEngine.UI;

public class SplashScreen : MonoBehaviour
{
  public Image logo;
  Color logoColor;
  public lerpMultiplier = 0.02f;

  void Start ()
  {
    logoColor = new Color (1, 1, 1, 0);
    logo.color = logoColor;

    StartCoroutine (GotoMainMenu ());
  }

  IEnumerator GotoMainMenu ()
  {
    yield return new WaitForSeconds (4);
    Application.LoadLevel ("MainMenu");
  }

  void Update ()
```

```
{
    logoColor = Color.Lerp(logoColor, new Color(1, 1, 1, 1),
    Time.time * lerpMultiplier);
    logo.color = logoColor;
}
```

Designing the user interface structure

Since we have already done the splash screen, let's dive into the main menu! The previous flow chart doesn't actually explain anything about how the main menu should function. Therefore, we need to design another flow chart to explain the structure of the main menu.

Our game is really simple, so we don't have many buttons on the menu—just simple start game and quit game buttons. By clicking on the different buttons, it will bring us to another user interface that does a different thing. We need to brainstorm all these details and put them into the flow chart.

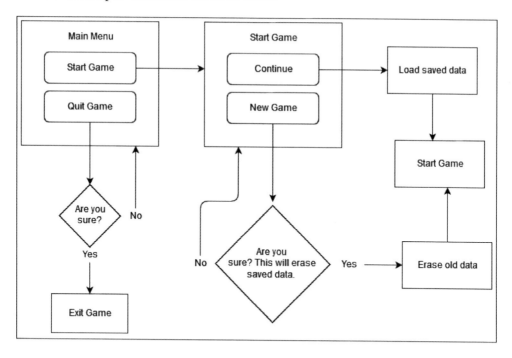

After you have done that, we will move over to Unity again and start designing our main menu based on the preceding flow chart. First, create a new scene called MainMenu, because the name of the scene has to match the name specified in the Application.LoadLevel() function in our previous script.

The first thing we see right after the splash screen is a menu with two buttons: **Start Game** and **Quit Game**, which are contained in a panel object. Above it is the game logo. The way to construct the main menu is quite similar to the splash screen, except an additional panel object and two buttons are added to the user interface.

The panel can be created by going to **Game Object | UI | Panel**, and the buttons can be added by going to **Game Object | UI | Button**. It's pretty simple and straightforward. You can change the button text by expanding the button from the hierarchy, and you will now see a text object under the button. Select it and you will be able to change the text on the **Inspector** panel. Subsequently, you can delete the text object, if you are going for a fully graphical type of button.

Below are the other menus that are present in the flow chart. At this moment, the user interface is not yet functional, but you have to be aware of their functionality and why it's being added to the UI in the first place. If you have any doubts or are questioning the design, it's never too late to go back to the flow chart and make some changes.

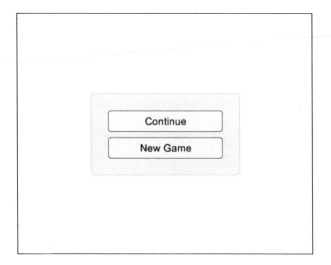

Each of these menus is contained in a separate canvas, which makes it easy to show and hide the entire menu from the script. You can try it in the Unity Editor by selecting one of the canvases and checking/unchecking the checkbox located beside the object name on the **Inspector** panel. You will see the entire menu disappear and reappear when you do that. More on this will be covered later in the chapter.

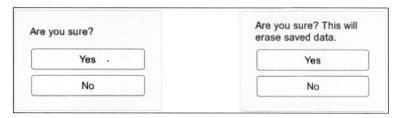

Once everything has been confirmed and all the required UI elements have been put in place, we will start writing the code to make it functional!

In Unity, create a new C# script called `MainMenu.cs`. This time, we are not manipulating the color or anything related to the UI elements, so we don't have to include the `UnityEngine.UI` dependency. However, we will activate and deactivate different canvases based on the state of the UI. To do that, we need to declare four variables to store the pointers to all the different menus for later use.

```
public GameObject mainMenuUI;
public GameObject startGameUI;
public GameObject exitGameUI;
public GameObject newGameUI;
```

Make sure they are public so that it will appear on the **Inspector** panel in the Unity Editor. Next, we only want the first menu to appear when the scene is loaded, and not the others. One way to do this is to make sure that only the first menu is shown and the rest are hidden before building the game, but sometimes we tend to be careless, so in order to avoid such a problem, we manually set it in the Start() function.

```
void Start ()
{
    mainMenuUI.SetActive (true);
    startGameUI.SetActive (false);
    exitGameUI.SetActive (false);
    newGameUI.SetActive (false);
}
```

After that, we have to create several functions that will be called by each of the buttons when pressed. What the functions do are mostly switch between different UIs by calling the SetActive() function to turn on or turn off the canvases. It's very easy to do this if we have designed the flow chart early on and have just followed it. This is why it's very important to make sure the flow chart is correct before we start writing any code.

The full code is here:

```
using UnityEngine;
using System.Collections;

public class MainMenu : MonoBehaviour
{
    public GameObject mainMenuUI;
    public GameObject startGameUI;
    public GameObject exitGameUI;
    public GameObject newGameUI;

    void Start ()
    {
        mainMenuUI.SetActive (true);
        startGameUI.SetActive (false);
        exitGameUI.SetActive (false);
        newGameUI.SetActive (false);
    }

    public void StartGamePressed ()
    {
        mainMenuUI.SetActive (false);
```

```
      startGameUI.SetActive (true);
    }

  public void QuitGamePressed ()
  {
    mainMenuUI.SetActive (false);
    exitGameUI.SetActive (true);
  }

  public void ContinuePressed ()
  {
    Application.LoadLevel ("Level01");
  }

  public void NewGamePressed ()
  {
    startGameUI.SetActive (false);
    newGameUI.SetActive (true);
  }

  public void QuitGameYesPressed ()
  {
    // Quit game and close the application
    Application.Quit ();
  }

  public void QuitGameNoPressed ()
  {
    exitGameUI.SetActive (false);
    mainMenuUI.SetActive (true);
  }

  public void NewGameYesPressed ()
  {
    // Jump to game level
    Application.LoadLevel ("Level01");
  }

  public void NewGameNoPressed ()
  {
    newGameUI.SetActive (false);
    startGameUI.SetActive (true);
  }
}
```

For now, both the **Continue** and **New Game** buttons will bring the player to the game scene without loading any saved data. This is because we will only learn how to save progression in the next chapter. Stay tuned.

To hook up the buttons to the preceding functions, select one of the buttons and scroll down to the bottom of the **Inspector** panel. There you will see a column with a label called **On Click()**. Then, click on the **+** button and drag the game object that has the MainMenu script attached to the input field. Then, click on the combo box on the right side and select the function that you want to call when the button is clicked. This is a really handy feature in Unity.

Once you are done setting all the buttons in the main menu scene, let's move on to the pause menu. If you refer back to the game structure, you will see a pause menu in the flow chart that can be accessed from the in-game scene. That particular flow chart, however, never explained how the pause menu actually works. Therefore, we need to create another flow chart just for the pause menu. Most of the things in the pause menu are similar to the main menu, except this time, we have to deal with keyboard input because the pause menu will be triggered when the player presses the **Escape** button on the keyboard.

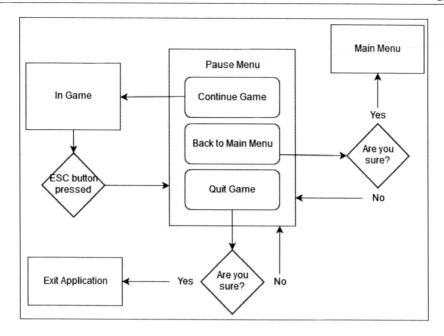

As for constructing the user interface, the steps are also very similar to the previous UI. The only difference now is that the background image is in black with 50% transparency. This is because we want the player to still be able to look at the 3D scene in the background when the game is paused.

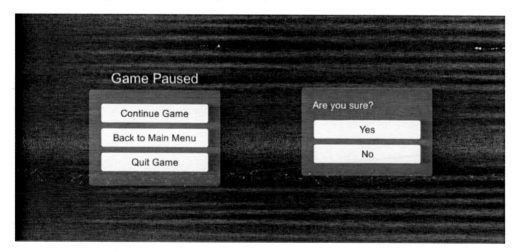

For the coding part, it's very similar to the main menu as well—switching between different canvases when clicking on the buttons. This time, however, we have two confirmation dialogs that look exactly the same but gog to different states when the buttons are pressed. We don't want to create the same UI twice, so instead we make use of enumeration (or enum for short) in C# to check which state we should navigate to when clicking on the buttons on the dialog.

First, create a new C# script called `PauseMenu.cs`. Then, at the top of your script, declare an enumeration called `mode`, which consists of two members: `mainMenu` and `quit`. Enumeration is essentially a way to assign a meaningful name to a set of integers so that programmers can easily remember it when writing code.

```
enum mode { mainMenu, quit };
```

Inside your `PauseMenu` class, declare two variables for the UI pointers and an integer variable called `selectedMode`. We will set this variable when a button is pressed to call out the confirmation dialog. This way, we will know which state it's going to navigate when the button on the dialog is pressed.

```
public GameObject pauseMenuUI;
public GameObject confirmUI;
mode selectedMode;
```

In the `Start()` function, again, manually display the first canvas and hide the other one to avoid a careless mistake.

```
void Start ()
{
   pauseMenuUI.SetActive (false);
   confirmUI.SetActive (false);
}
```

In the `Update()` function, we check whether the *Esc* key is pressed by calling `Input.GetKeyDown()` and insert `KeyCode.Escape` as the input variable. The function will return `true` if the *Esc* key is pressed, and thus pausing the game.

There are many ways to pause a game. The simplest method is to just stop the in-game time by setting the time scale to zero. This way, everything will be frozen, including all animations, special effects, and game logic that relies on in-game time. By setting the time scale back to one, the game will continue as it is.

Another thing that I have added to the pause menu script is unlocking the game cursor and unhiding it when the game resumes. This is because later in this chapter, I will be hiding the game cursor when constructing character movement. More on this will be covered later.

```
void Update ()
```

```
    {
        if (Input.GetKeyDown (KeyCode.Escape))
        {
            if (Time.timeScale == 1)
            {
                Time.timeScale = 0;
                pauseMenuUI.SetActive (true);

                Cursor.lockState = CursorLockMode.None;
                Cursor.visible = true;
            }
            else
            {
                Time.timeScale = 1;
                pauseMenuUI.SetActive (false);

                Cursor.lockState = CursorLockMode.Locked;
                Cursor.visible = false;
            }
        }
    }
}
```

Now, I will explain a little bit about the usage of enumeration we declared earlier in this script. If we refer back to the flow chart, we can see that the confirmation menu is used to navigate to two different states: one to the main menu, and another one to quit the game completely.

Therefore, when the **Back to Main Menu** button is pressed, we need to set the selectedMode variable to mainMenu before activating the confirmation dialog.

```
public void BackMainMenuPressed()
{
    selectedMode = mode.mainMenu;

    pauseMenuUI.SetActive (false);
    confirmUI.SetActive (true);
}
```

The same goes for the **Quit Game** button. Set the selectedMode variable to quit before showing the dialog.

```
public void QuitGamePressed()
{
    selectedMode = mode.quit;

    pauseMenuUI.SetActive (false);
```

```
        confirmUI.SetActive (true);
    }
```

Thus, when clicking on the **Yes** button on the **confirmation** dialog, we must check the `selectedMode` variable and trigger the relevant action accordingly, which in this case, is loading the main menu scene `if selectedMode is mainmenu` and quitting the game completely if otherwise.

```
    public void YesPressed()
    {
      if (selectedMode == mode.mainMenu)
      {
        Application.LoadLevel("MainMenu");
      }
      else
      {
        Application.Quit();
      }
    }
```

The full code is here:

```
    using UnityEngine;
    using System.Collections;

    enum mode { mainMenu, quit };

    public class PauseMenu : MonoBehaviour
    {
      public GameObject pauseMenuUI;
      public GameObject confirmUI;
      mode selectedMode;

      void Start ()
      {
        pauseMenuUI.SetActive (false);
        confirmUI.SetActive (false);
      }

      void Update ()
      {
        if (Input.GetKeyDown (KeyCode.Escape))
        {
          if (Time.timeScale == 1)
          {
```

```
      Time.timeScale = 0;
      pauseMenuUI.SetActive (true);

      Cursor.lockState = CursorLockMode.None;
      Cursor.visible = true;
    }
    else
    {
      Time.timeScale = 1;
      pauseMenuUI.SetActive (false);

      Cursor.lockState = CursorLockMode.Locked;
      Cursor.visible = false;
    }
  }
}

public void ContinueGamePressed()
{
  Time.timeScale = 1;
  pauseMenuUI.SetActive (false);
}

public void BackMainMenuPressed()
{
  selectedMode = mode.mainMenu;

  pauseMenuUI.SetActive (false);
  confirmUI.SetActive (true);
}

public void QuitGamePressed()
{
  selectedMode = mode.quit;

  pauseMenuUI.SetActive (false);
  confirmUI.SetActive (true);
}

public void YesPressed()
{
  if (selectedMode == mode.mainMenu)
  {
    Application.LoadLevel("MainMenu");
```

```
        }
        else
        {
            Application.Quit();
        }
    }

    public void NoPressed()
    {
        confirmUI.SetActive (false);
        pauseMenuUI.SetActive (true);
    }
}
```

Player inputs and character movements

We are now done constructing the basic user interface. Now, let's move on to player inputs and character movements! A game character, especially the one who gets controlled by the player, usually contains tons of different states, such as idling, running, attack, and so on, which changes frequently based on the mix of player inputs and other conditions, such as health point, timer, and so on.

The following is an example of a basic character structure displayed in a flow chart:

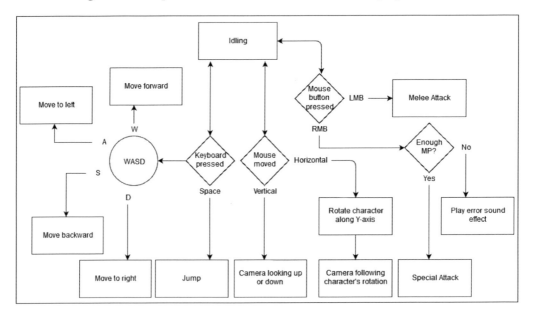

In Unity, there are many ways to move an object or a character, such as adjusting the variables of the transform directly, or applying force to a rigid body, or using a navigation mesh agent to automatically calculate the shortest path, and so on. In this case, we would need to use the character controller instead, which can be found at **Component | Physics | Character Controller**. After adding the character controller component to your game character, we can start writing the code. We will create a new C# script called `PlayerMovement.cs`.

First of all, there are several variables that we need to declare, such as the walking speed, jumping strength, value for acceleration, and so on, which will be used to simulate the movements later on. Besides that, we also need to declare the `CharacterController` variable in order for us to use it to apply motion to the character.

```
public float walkSpeed = 5;
public float walkSideSpeed = 3;
public float walkReverseSpeed = 2;
public float rotateSpeed = 100;
public float jumpStrength = 0.4f;

Vector3 walkAcceleration = new Vector3(0, 0, 0);
float jumpAcceleration = 0;
int jumpCount = 0;


public CharacterController playerController;
public Animator playerAnimator;
```

Next, we create two custom functions: `KeyboardInputs()` and `Movements()` — to separate the code to avoid messy code. This way, we can manage and debug the code easily without having to scroll through the script and wonder which part of the code does what.

```
void Update ()
{
  KeyboardInputs();
  Movements();

  // Pass the movement speed to animator for switching between
  animation states
  playerAnimator.SetFloat("runningSpeed",
  walkAcceleration.magnitude);
  playerAnimator.SetFloat("jumpingSpeed", jumpAcceleration);

}
```

We will start writing the Movements() function first. The logic is actually quite simple: we use the Move() function in the character controller to move it on every single tick. However, we control the value of the walkAcceleration variable to move or stop the character. It's like a car engine that is always turned on and running, but only when you lock in the gear will the car start moving. For example, if walkAcceleration is set to Vector3(0, 0, 0), the character will not move, even if the Move() function is being executed on every tick.

```
// Horizontol movements
playerController.Move(walkAcceleration * Time.deltaTime);

// Vertical movements
playerController.Move(new Vector3(0, jumpAcceleration, 0));
```

Time.deltaTime refers to **delta time** or **delta timing**; it's a variable that tells you how many milliseconds have passed between the last frame and the current frame. Delta time is used to add up the speed of moving objects so that it all move at a consistent speed across different computers despite running at different frame rates. We also call this framerate-independent motion or time-based motion. In Unity, the value of delta time is provided by the game engine at every frame, which you can use in the form of a variable by typing Time.deltaTime.

In this script, we have executed the Move() function twice in every tick: one for walking (horizontal movements) and another one for jumping (vertical movements). At the same time, the character's rotation is also being adjusted based on the mouse's movement along the *X* axis. The mouse movement can be obtained by calling Input.GetAxis("Mouse X") and specifying the axis you want.

```
// Rotation
playerController.transform.Rotate(new Vector3(0,
Input.GetAxis("Mouse X"), 0) * Time.deltaTime * rotateSpeed);
```

Besides acceleration during movements, we also have to write the code for deceleration. In real life, nothing stops instantly, especially when no external force is applied to the moving object. Many newbie programmers always make the same mistake—stopping the character instantly when the keyboard button is not pressed. This looks OK when the character is walking on the ground, but it will look very unnatural if the character is jumping or falling in the air.

To solve this issue, we need to check if the character is standing on the ground by checking the variable in the character controller called isGrounded. If the character is in the air, slowly decrease the walkAcceleration vector over time using a function from the Vector3 class called MoveTowards(), which interpolates a given vector to a target value over a period of time. This makes the falling movement look more realistic and fluid.

As for vertical deceleration, always adjust the jumpAcceleration variable back to -0.98, because that is the actual value of gravity. The jumpAcceleration variable, in this case, is not a vector but rather a floating point number. So, instead of using Vector3.MoveTowards(), we use Mathf.MoveTowards() instead.

```
// Horizontal deceleration
if (playerController.isGrounded)
{
   walkAcceleration = Vector3.zero;
   jumpCount = 0;
}
else
{
   walkAcceleration = Vector3.MoveTowards(walkAcceleration,
   Vector3.zero, Time.deltaTime);
}

// Vertical deceleration
if (jumpAcceleration > -0.98f)
{
   jumpAcceleration = Mathf.MoveTowards(jumpAcceleration,
   -0.98f, Time.deltaTime * 2);
}
```

After that, we will learn how to write the code for player inputs. Like I mentioned previously, all the code for player inputs is written in the KeyboardInputs() function so that it's easier for us to look for the code.

Let's start from the WASD keys, which is considered standard in the games industry for first-person and third-person character movements. I will show you an example of the *W* key movement, which is moving the character forward. The rest are mostly similar to this code, the only differences being the key that is being pressed as well as the direction of the movements.

First off, we need to check if the character is on the ground or in the air. This is very important because when the character is walking on the ground, you need to keep on adding force to it because the friction of the ground will reduce the force over time. However, if the character is jumping or falling in the air, there is no friction that can cause it to slow down. In this case, if we keep on adding force to the character while in the air, he will fly away like a rocket, which is not what we want. Instead, we just need to apply a constant vector to it, and it will all look right.

```
if (Input.GetKey(KeyCode.W))
{
  // Prevent player to fly away like bullet when not on ground
  if (playerController.isGrounded)
  {
    walkAcceleration += playerController.transform.forward *
    walkSpeed;
  }
  else
  {
    walkAcceleration = playerController.transform.forward *
    walkSpeed;
  }
}
```

For other keys, such as *A*, *S*, and *D*, the only major difference is the movement direction, for which you just need to change `playerController.transform.forward` to `playerController.transform.right`, as well as making the plus-equal sign to minus-equal, depending on which direction you want it to move.

You can check out the following full code for further details:

```
using UnityEngine;
using System.Collections;

public class PlayerMovement : MonoBehaviour
{
  public float walkSpeed = 5;
  public float walkSideSpeed = 3;
  public float walkReverseSpeed = 2;
  public float rotateSpeed = 100;
  public float jumpStrength = 0.4f;

  Vector3 walkAcceleration = new Vector3(0, 0, 0);
  float jumpAcceleration = 0;
```

```
    int jumpCount = 0;

    public CharacterController playerController;
    public Animator playerAnimator;

    void Update ()
    {
      KeyboardInputs();
      Movements();

// Pass the movement speed to animator for switching
  between animation states
  playerAnimator.SetFloat("runningSpeed",
  walkAcceleration.magnitude);
  playerAnimator.SetFloat("jumpingSpeed", jumpAcceleration);
  }

    void KeyboardInputs()
    {
      if (Input.GetKey(KeyCode.W))
      {
        // Prevent player to fly away like bullet when not on ground
        if (playerController.isGrounded)
        {
          walkAcceleration += playerController.transform.
          forward * walkSpeed;
        }
        else
        {
          walkAcceleration = playerController.transform.forward
          * walkSpeed;
        }
      }

      if (Input.GetKey(KeyCode.A))
      {
        // Prevent player to fly away like bullet when not on ground
        if (playerController.isGrounded)
        {
          walkAcceleration += playerController.transform.right
          * -walkSideSpeed;
        }
        else
```

```
    {
      walkAcceleration = playerController.transform.right
      * -walkSideSpeed;
    }
  }
}

if (Input.GetKey(KeyCode.S))
{
  // Prevent player to fly away like bullet when not on ground
  if (playerController.isGrounded)
  {
    walkAcceleration += playerController.transform.forward
    * -walkReverseSpeed;
  }
  else
  {
    walkAcceleration = playerController.transform.forward
    * -walkReverseSpeed;
  }
}

if (Input.GetKey(KeyCode.D))
{
  // Prevent player to fly away like bullet when not on ground
  if (playerController.isGrounded)
  {
    walkAcceleration += playerController.transform.right
    * walkSideSpeed;
  }
  else
  {
    walkAcceleration = playerController.transform.right
    * walkSideSpeed;
  }
}

if (Input.GetKeyDown(KeyCode.Space))
{
  // Double jump
  if (jumpCount < 2)
  {
    jumpAcceleration = jumpStrength;
```

```
            jumpCount += 1;
        }
    }
}

void Movements()
{
    // Horizontol movements
    playerController.Move(walkAcceleration * Time.deltaTime);

    // Vertical movements
    playerController.Move(new Vector3(0, jumpAcceleration, 0));

    // Rotation
    playerController.transform.Rotate(new Vector3(0,
    Input.GetAxis("Mouse X"), 0) * Time.deltaTime * rotateSpeed);

    // Horizontal deceleration
    if (playerController.isGrounded)
    {
        walkAcceleration = Vector3.zero;
        jumpCount = 0;
    }
    else
    {
        walkAcceleration = Vector3.MoveTowards(walkAcceleration,
        Vector3.zero, Time.deltaTime);
    }

    // Vertical deceleration
    if (jumpAcceleration > -0.98f)
    {
        jumpAcceleration = Mathf.MoveTowards(jumpAcceleration,
        -0.98f, Time.deltaTime * 2);
    }
    }
}
```

Now that our character can finally move, there is one more thing that we need to settle—camera movement. We need a camera that follows the character around so that we can see where our character is going. However, before we start writing the code, we must set up our camera properly so that it is compatible with the method we used in the code.

You need to create three empty game objects and place them exactly where the character is standing. Then, rename the objects as `Position`, `Yaw`, and `Pitch`. After that, make `Yaw` the child of `Position`, `Pitch` the child of `Yaw`, and finally make the game camera the child of `Pitch`. Keep all three empty objects where they are, but move the game camera to where you want it to be, in this case, behind the character. It may seem confusing at the moment, but you will understand later on when I start explaining in detail.

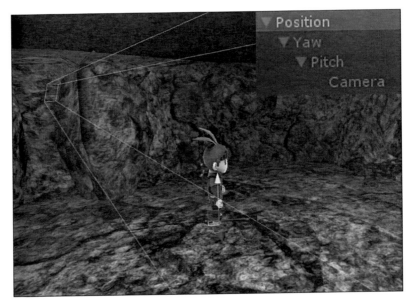

Basically, the `Position` object will follow the character's position wherever he goes. It is simply interpolating its position to the character's pivot point, which is located between the feet. Next, the `Yaw` object will handle the yaw rotation, and the `Pitch` object will handle the pitch rotation. By separating the rotation handling to different objects, we can avoid mathematical problems caused by Euler angles. Lastly, because the camera is the child of all three objects, the position and rotation are all inherited to the camera, resulting in a smooth and fluid camera movement.

Therefore, when we start writing the camera code, we need to declare the pointers to the player's transform, the `Yaw` object as well as the `Pitch` object, so that we can include them into the movement calculations. Other than that, we also need to declare some variables such as movement speed and rotation speed. Let's create a C# script called `PlayerCamera.cs` and then declare all the public variables:

```
public bool lockCursor = true;
public float followSpeed = 10;
```

```
public float yawSpeed = 10;
public float pitchSpeed = 50;

public Transform playerTransform;
public Transform yawPivot;
public Transform pitchPivot;
```

After that, in the `Start()` function, we ask Unity to hide and lock the game cursor so that we can move the camera around using the mouse without getting stopped when the mouse reaches the edge of the screen.

```
void Start ()
{
  if (lockCursor)
  {
    Cursor.lockState = CursorLockMode.Locked;
    Cursor.visible = false;
  }
}
```

Then, inside the `Update()` function, there are three things that we need to do: move the `Position` object to where the player is located, rotate the `Yaw` object based on where the character is facing, and rotate the `Pitch` object based on the mouse movement along the *y* axis.

```
transform.position = Vector3.Lerp(transform.position,
playerTransform.position, Time.deltaTime * followSpeed);

Vector3 yawRotation = yawPivot.localRotation.eulerAngles;
yawRotation.y = Mathf.LerpAngle (yawRotation.y,
playerTransform.localRotation.eulerAngles.y, Time.deltaTime *
yawSpeed);
yawPivot.localRotation = Quaternion.Euler (yawRotation);

Vector3 pitchRotation = pitchPivot.localRotation.eulerAngles;
pitchRotation.x -= Input.GetAxis ("Mouse Y") * Time.deltaTime
* pitchSpeed;
pitchPivot.localRotation = Quaternion.Euler (pitchRotation);
```

Lastly, we need to limit the `Pitch` object's rotation so that we will not get an inverted camera view if we move the mouse too much along the *y* axis.

```
// Limit the angle
if (pitchPivot.localRotation.eulerAngles.x > 55 &&
pitchPivot.localRotation.eulerAngles.x < 90)
{
  pitchRotation = pitchPivot.localRotation.eulerAngles;
```

```
      pitchRotation.x = 55;
      pitchPivot.localRotation = Quaternion.Euler (pitchRotation);
   }
   else if (pitchPivot.localRotation.eulerAngles.x < 335 &&
   pitchPivot.localRotation.eulerAngles.x > 90)
   {
     pitchRotation = pitchPivot.localRotation.eulerAngles;
     pitchRotation.x = 335;
     pitchPivot.localRotation = Quaternion.Euler (pitchRotation);
   }
```

This is the full code:

```
   using UnityEngine;
   using System.Collections;

   public class PlayerCamera : MonoBehaviour
   {
     public bool lockCursor = true;
     public float followSpeed = 10;
     public float yawSpeed = 10;
     public float pitchSpeed = 50;

     public Transform playerTransform;
     public Transform yawPivot;
     public Transform pitchPivot;

     void Start ()
     {
       if (lockCursor)
       {
         Cursor.lockState = CursorLockMode.Locked;
         Cursor.visible = false;
       }
     }

     void Update ()
     {
       transform.position = Vector3.Lerp(transform.position,
       playerTransform.position, Time.deltaTime * followSpeed);

       Vector3 yawRotation = yawPivot.localRotation.eulerAngles;
       yawRotation.y = Mathf.LerpAngle (yawRotation.y,
       playerTransform.localRotation.eulerAngles.y, Time.deltaTime
       * yawSpeed);
```

```
yawPivot.localRotation = Quaternion.Euler (yawRotation);

Vector3 pitchRotation = pitchPivot.localRotation.eulerAngles;
pitchRotation.x -= Input.GetAxis ("Mouse Y") *
Time.deltaTime * pitchSpeed;
pitchPivot.localRotation = Quaternion.Euler (pitchRotation);

// Limit the angle
if (pitchPivot.localRotation.eulerAngles.x > 55
&& pitchPivot.localRotation.eulerAngles.x < 90)
{
  pitchRotation = pitchPivot.localRotation.eulerAngles;
  pitchRotation.x = 55;
  pitchPivot.localRotation = Quaternion.Euler (pitchRotation);
}
else if (pitchPivot.localRotation.eulerAngles.x < 335 &&
pitchPivot.localRotation.eulerAngles.x > 90)
{
  pitchRotation = pitchPivot.localRotation.eulerAngles;
  pitchRotation.x = 335;
  pitchPivot.localRotation = Quaternion.Euler (pitchRotation);
}
}
}
```

Finally, we can move our character around in the level! How cool is that!

Now that we can move our character around, what should we do next? Attack, of course!

The reason why I chose to teach how to do a melee attack instead of shooting projectiles is because there are simply too many tutorials out there that focus on shooting projectiles, but hardly any teach you how to do short-range combat.

There are, of course, many different ways to do a melee attack, depending on how sophisticated you want it to be. However, in our case, we just want a normal melee attack, which basically detects who is near to the player and who is not. Then, when the player is doing the attack, apply the damages to those who are standing nearby. This is actually not as difficult as you might think.

But before that, let's create the flow chart for the melee attack so that we are really clear about how the attack should be done.

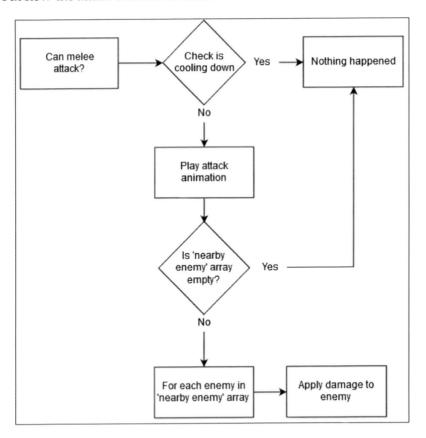

From the preceding flow chart, you will notice there is a cool down after every attack. This is to avoid the player from doing multiple attacks by clicking the left mouse button multiple times in a row. It makes sure that the player can only make a single attack between every interval. Do notice that I will not be showing how to implement the special attack because it will be shown in the next chapter. Stay tuned.

Then, you also notice that there is something called **nearby enemy array** in the flow chart. This array is basically a list used to record which monster is nearby, ignoring those that are far away. When the player is doing the melee attack, only the monsters that are registered in the array will be damaged.

So, the first thing when we write the code is to declare all the variables needed for later use, such as the hit point, cool down interval, and the `nearbyEnemy` array:

```
public float attackDamage = 10;
public float attackCooldownInterval = 1;
float attackCooldownTime = 0;

ArrayList nearbyEnemy;
```

Next, we must create the array in the `Start()` function; otherwise, you will not be able to use it later.

```
void Start ()
{
   nearbyEnemy = new ArrayList ();
}
```

After that, we detect whether any monster is standing in front of the character by using the built-in function called `OnTriggerEnter()`. This function will only work if you have a trigger attached to the character. Add the trigger box to your character if you have not done it. When the function is triggered, it will tell you which object is colliding with it, so you can then check if it's a monster by comparing its tag. If the object is indeed a monster, add it to the `nearbyEnemy` array:

```
void OnTriggerEnter (Collider col)
{
   // Add nearby enemy to array if within attack distance
   if (col.tag == "Monster")
   {
      nearbyEnemy.Add (col.gameObject);
   }
}
```

However, if a monster is too far away and is now outside the trigger box, do a `for` loop to check each of the objects registered with the `nearbyEnemy` array. Then, remove it from the array if it matches the monster that left the trigger box:

```
void OnTriggerExit (Collider col)
{
  // Remove enemy from array if not within attack distance
  if (col.tag == "Monster")
  {
    for (int i = 0; i < nearbyEnemy.Count; i++)
    {
      if (nearbyEnemy[i] == col.gameObject)
      {
        nearbyEnemy.RemoveAt(i);
      }
    }
  }
}
```

Finally, in the `Update()` function, we detect if the left mouse button is clicked by calling `Input.GetMouseButtonDown(0)`. Then, we check if it's still cooling down or ready for the next attack by comparing the game's total elapsed second — `Time.time` with the `attackCooldownTime` variable. Whenever we successfully made a single attack, we must set the `attackCooldownTime` variable to the future time, by adding the current game time with `attackCooldownInterval`.

For example, if the current game time (total elapsed seconds) is at 1000th second, and `attackCooldownInterval` is 1, that means `attackCooldownTime` will be at the 1001st second, and the player will not be able to make the next attack until 1 second later.

To apply damages to nearby enemies, simply loop through the `nearbyEnemy` array and call the `GetDamage()` function, which we will create later in this chapter.

```
void Update ()
{
  if (Input.GetMouseButtonDown(0))
  {
    if (Time.time > attackCooldownTime)
    {
      if (nearbyEnemy.Count > 0)
      {
        // Apply damage to all nearby enemies
        for (int i = 0; i < nearbyEnemy.Count; i++)
```

```
        {
          (nearbyEnemy[i] as GameObject).GetComponent<EnemyAI>().
          GetDamage(attackDamage);
        }
      }

      // Set cool down time
      attackCooldownTime = Time.time + attackCooldownInterval;
    }
  }
}
```

The full code for the melee attack is shown next:

```
using UnityEngine;
using System.Collections;

public class PlayerAttack : MonoBehaviour
{
  public float attackDamage = 10;
  public float attackCooldownInterval = 1;
  float attackCooldownTime = 0;

  ArrayList nearbyEnemy;

  void Start ()
  {
    nearbyEnemy = new ArrayList ();
  }

  void Update ()
  {
    if (Input.GetMouseButtonDown(0))
    {
      if (Time.time > attackCooldownTime)
      {
        if (nearbyEnemy.Count > 0)
        {
          // Apply damage to all nearby enemies
          for (int i = 0; i < nearbyEnemy.Count; i++)
          {
            (nearbyEnemy[i] as GameObject).GetComponent<EnemyAI>
            ().GetDamage(attackDamage);
          }
```

```
            }

        // Set cool down time
        attackCooldownTime = Time.time + attackCooldownInterval;
        }
      }
    }

    void OnTriggerEnter (Collider col)
    {
      // Add nearby enemy to array if within attack distance
      if (col.tag == "Monster")
      {
        nearbyEnemy.Add(col.gameObject);
      }
    }

    void OnTriggerExit (Collider col)
    {
      // Remove enemy from array if not within attack distance
      if (col.tag == "Monster")
      {
        for (int i = 0; i < nearbyEnemy.Count; i++)
        {
          if (nearbyEnemy[i] == col.gameObject)
          {
            nearbyEnemy.RemoveAt(i);
          }
        }
      }
    }
  }
```

Creating basic artificial intelligence

Phew, we have come a long way, haven't we? But the most exciting part is just about to start—we will learn how to create basic game AI in Unity!

In a nutshell, artificial intelligence is all about making decisions autonomously based on a set of conditions and requirements. If a given condition has been met, then the AI will try to move from its current state to the other state that fits the criteria. This is what we call the **finite state machine**.

In order to know what conditions we need to set in our AI and what decisions it can make, we will design yet another flow chart for the AI:

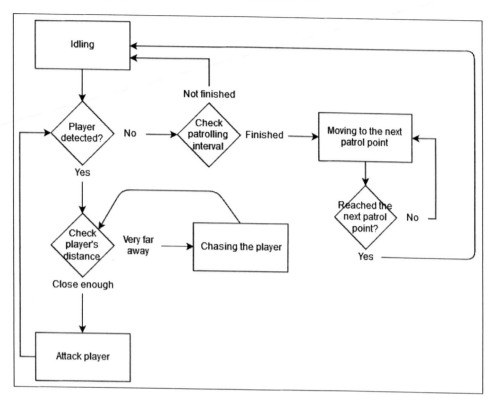

In this chapter, we will only focus on the part where the AI will start chasing the player whenever the player is nearby. We will learn how to make the AI patrol around a given area in the next chapter, so stay tuned.

Before we start writing the code, we need to add a component called **Nav Mesh Agent** to our monster prefab. Without this component, our monster will lose the ability to find the shortest path and move toward the player.

After that, we will create a C# script called `EnemyAI` and attach it to our monster prefab. We will start writing the code by declaring the variables needed by the script:

```
public NavMeshAgent agent;
public float healthPoint = 50;
public Animator animator;
GameObject player;
```

Then, in the `Start()` function, we will find the player by calling `GameObject.FindWithTag()` and save it to the `player` variable. Since there is only one player in the entire scene, it's OK to search through the entire scene to find the player when the game started. Do not, however, use this function in the `Update()` function because that will greatly slow down the performance of the game.

After that, in the `Update()` function, we will calculate the distance between the monster and the player character. If the player is nearby, then the monster will start chasing him by calling the `SetDestination()` function from the Nav Mesh Agent.

```
void Update ()
{
  if (player != null)
  {
    // Check if player is nearby
    if (Vector3.Distance(transform.position,
    player.transform.position) <= 6)
    {
      // Move toward player
      agent.SetDestination(player.transform.position);
      // Pass the movement velocity to animator
      animator.SetFloat("runningSpeed", agent.velocity.magnitude);
    }
  }
}
```

Finally, we also create the `GetDamage()` function that was used previously in the melee attack script so that the Unity compiler will no longer display an error that says `GetDamage()` function not found. In this function, we will deduct the health points of the monster and check if the health point has reached zero. If it does, it will be removed from the scene by calling the `Destroy()` function:

```
public void GetDamage (float damage)
{
  healthPoint -= damage;

  if (healthPoint <= 0)
  {
    Die ();
  }
}


void Die ()
```

```
{
  Destroy (gameObject);
}
```

The following is the full code for the artificial intelligence:

```
using UnityEngine;
using System.Collections;

public class EnemyAI : MonoBehaviour
{
  public NavMeshAgent agent;
  public float healthPoint = 50;
  public Animator animator;
  GameObject player;

  void Start ()
  {
    // Find player
    player = GameObject.FindWithTag ("Player");
  }

  void Update ()
  {
    if (player != null)
    {
      // Check if player is nearby
      if (Vector3.Distance(transform.position,
      player.transform.position) <= 6)
      {
        // Move toward player
        agent.SetDestination(player.transform.position);
        // Pass the movement velocity to animator
        animator.SetFloat("runningSpeed", agent.velocity.magnitude);
      }
    }
  }

  public void GetDamage (float damage)
  {
    healthPoint -= damage;

    if (healthPoint <= 0)
```

```
        {
            Die ();
        }
    }

    void Die ()
    {
        Destroy (gameObject);
    }
}
```

Before the monsters are able to chase the player, you need to open up the navigation panel by going to **Window | Navigation** and click on the **Bake** button on top, and then click again on the **Bake** button in the lower-right corner. After several seconds, you will see blue polygons being generated all over the level. These blue polygons are what we call navigation meshes and are used by the Nav Mesh Agent to calculate path finding.

These are the options for navigation mesh baking:

- **Agent Radius**: This option defines how close the bake agent can get to a wall or a ledge.

- **Agent Height**: **Agent Height** determines the height that can be reached by the bake agent.

- **Max Slope**: This defines how steep the ramps are that the bake agent walk up.

- **Step Height**: This determines how high the obstructions are that the bake agent can step on.

- **Drop Height**: This parameter controls what is the highest distance for the bake agent to link two off-link meshes for dropping.

- **Jump Distance**: This determines the further distance for the bake agent to link two off-link meshes for jumping.

- **Manual Voxel Size**: By enabling this option, you can manually set the accuracy of the baking process by changing the voxel size.

- **Voxel Size**: The default setting resulting in 3 voxels per agent radius, which means the whole agent width is 6 voxel. Changing this value will affect both the accuracy as well as the baking speed.

- **Min Region Area**: Using this, regions that have a surface area smaller than the specified value will be removed.

- **Height Mesh**: By enabling this option, you can get a more accurate placement of your character on the navmesh surface, However, this will take up more memory and processing at runtime, and it will also take a little longer to bake the mesh.

Once you have generated the navigation meshes, try duplicating the monster prefabs across the level, and have fun getting chased by them!

Summary

In this chapter, you have learned how to design your game structures with flow charts and implement them in the Unity Engine. You have also learned how to create a basic user interface in Unity, how to make your game character move around, and how to create basic AI that can chase you around in your game.

In the next chapter, we will walk you through how to create game progression and start building some power-ups!

7
Creating Levels and Game Progression

In this chapter, we will discuss how to create player stats and alter it through power-up items. We will also discuss how to create a more advanced enemy AI that is able to patrol randomly in the game level, as well as how to create save points that can be used by the players to save their game progression.

In this chapter, we will cover the following:

- Creating character attributes
- Adding in-game items and power-ups
- Improving enemy AI
- Adding save points

Creating character attributes

In the previous chapter, we learned how to create a lively in-game character that is able to move around based on the player's input. However, this is not enough to make your game fun and addictive. There is no standard definition on what makes a game fun. However, by observing successful titles that have been proven (from the sales figure) to be fun, we can easily find one similarity between these games — they all have a well-planned progression throughout the game.

The key behind a good progression is to let the players learn and improve their playing skill over time while facing greater challenges in every new level. Besides this, players should also be given larger rewards to solve a difficult puzzle or quest, which creates a satisfactory feeling that will keep the player coming back for bigger rewards.

Game rewards can be divided into several different types and categories. One of the most familiar is the player's level. Every level up will increase the strength, speed, or other attribute of the player character, and hence allowing it to challenge stronger enemies. Besides this, one of the other types of reward is to give in-game items to the player, such as a new weapon, new equipment, and so on, which also increases the attributes of the player character. This not only makes it stronger but also changes the outlook of the character.

Another type of reward is unlocking features that are hidden away from the player before he/she has reached a certain level or achieved a specific goal. Examples of locked features are special skills, extra movements (double jump, dash, and so on), or special ability that allows the player to enter a path that he/she wouldn't be able to do so previously—for example, crossing a broken bridge by unlocking the flying ability.

To create player attributes in Unity, first let's create the C# script named `PlayerAttribute.cs`. This script only serves as a container for the attributes and contains no logic in it.

```
using UnityEngine;
using System.Collections;

public class PlayerAttribute : MonoBehaviour
{
  public int level = 1;
  public float healthPoint = 100;
  public float manaPoint = 0;
  public float attackDamage = 10;
  public float specialAttackDamage = 50;
  public float defense = 2;
}
```

The preceding code is pretty self-explanatory. The script is used to save the player's attributes, such as level, health point, hit point, and so on. Other scripts will have to access this script if it needs the player's attributes. I will try to explain this by adjusting the `PlayerAttack.cs` script that we created in the previous chapter. Since we have already accessed the `attackDamage` (hit point) attribute from the `PlayerAttribute` script, we can now remove this variable:

```
public float attackDamage = 10;
```

Replace it with the following:

```
public PlayerAttribute playerAttr;
```

After this, have a look at the following line:

```
(nearbyEnemy[i] as GameObject).GetComponent<EnemyAI>
().GetDamage(attackDamage);
```

Change the preceding line to the following:

```
(nearbyEnemy[i] as GameObject).GetComponent<EnemyAI>().
GetDamage(playerAttr.attackDamage);
```

We have just removed the local variable `attackDamage` completely. When the player is trying to attack the monster enemy, the `playerAttack` script will use the `attackDamage` variable in the `playerAttribute` script instead.

Adding in-game items and power-ups

Next, you will learn how to alter the player's attributes by creating in-game items that can be picked up by the player. Let's create the prefab in the Unity Editor before proceeding to the script. I did a simple cross-shape prefab using boxes, removed the colliders from the boxes, and attached a sphere collider component to it, which are marked as a trigger. I also set its tag as `Item` so that we can use it later. The tag is a very useful functionality in Unity, which allows you to group game objects into the same category for your scripts to identify them during gameplay. For example, you might define `Player` and `Enemy` tags for player-controlled characters and non-player characters respectively.

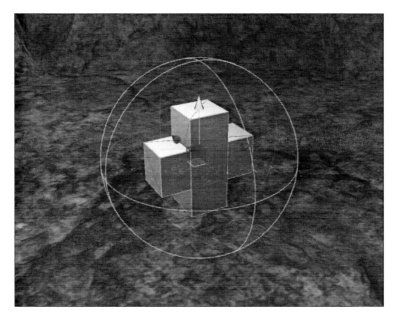

Instead of creating an individual script for every item of different purpose, we can create one universal power-up script that alters different player attributes depending on how we set the variables.

Therefore, the first thing we need to add to the power-up script is to define all the variables of the item:

```
public float addHealthPoint = 0;
public float addManaPoint = 0;
public float addAttackDamage = 0;
public float addSpecialAttackDamage = 0;
public float addDefense = 0;
```

By default, all these variables are set to zero. Developers can then apply this script to an item prefab and set the values they want for a particular variable, which means if the player obtains this item, the variable(s) that is not zero will be added to the player's attributes of similar name; for instance, addHealthPoint will be added to player's healthPoint variable.

Next, we will detect whether the item is colliding with the player. If it does, the script will try to access to its PlayerAttribute script and alter the player's attributes. Last but not least, we need to destroy the item once it has done its job. Make sure that you have set the tag of your player as Player so that the following code will work properly:

```
void OnTriggerEnter (Collider col)
{
  if (col.tag == "Player")
  {
    PlayerAttribute playeAttr =
    col.gameObject.GetComponent<PlayerAttribute>();
    playeAttr.manaPoint += addManaPoint;
    playeAttr.healthPoint += addHealthPoint;
    playeAttr.attackDamage += addAttackDamage;
    playeAttr.specialAttackDamage += addSpecialAttackDamage;
    playeAttr.defense += addDefense;

    Destroy(gameObject);
  }
}
```

The full script looks like this:

```
using UnityEngine;
using System.Collections;

public class Powerup : MonoBehaviour
{
  public float addHealthPoint = 0;
```

```
public float addManaPoint = 0;
public float addAttackDamage = 0;
public float addSpecialAttackDamage = 0;
public float addDefense = 0;

void OnTriggerEnter (Collider col)
{
  if (col.tag == "Player")
  {
    PlayerAttribute playeAttr =
    col.gameObject.GetComponent<PlayerAttribute>();
    playeAttr.manaPoint += addManaPoint;
    playeAttr.healthPoint += addHealthPoint;
    playeAttr.attackDamage += addAttackDamage;
    playeAttr.specialAttackDamage += addSpecialAttackDamage;
    playeAttr.defense += addDefense;

    Destroy(gameObject);
  }
 }
}
```

Once we're done with the healing item, we will move on to create another type of item which restores the mana point. Since we have already written the item script that can be used to add different attributes, we can reuse the script and skip the coding part! What we need to do next is create the item prefab. Look at the following simple item prefab using several cylinders:

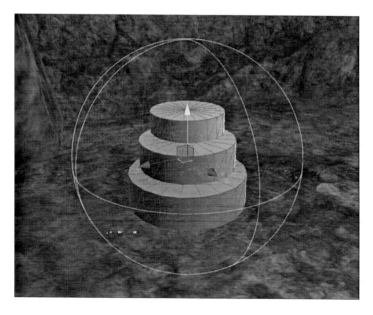

In order to test the effect of the item, we will create the special attack for the player! The special attack will be huge magic bullets shooting out from the player toward eight different directions. The special attack, however, requires the mana point to be full in order to trigger the attack.

First, we will create the prefab for the bullets. For this demo, I will just use a simple sphere created in Unity as follows:

Then, we will create a C# script named `BulletMovement.cs` and attach it to the prefab we have just created. Within the script, we will ask Unity to move the object toward its front direction and destroy the bullet after 5 seconds. The code looks like this:

```
using UnityEngine;
using System.Collections;

public class BulletMovement : MonoBehaviour
{
  void Start ()
  {
    StartCoroutine (DestroyBullet());
  }

  void Update ()
  {
    transform.position += transform.forward * Time.deltaTime * 5;
```

```
    }

    IEnumerator DestroyBullet ()
    {
        yield return new WaitForSeconds(5);
        Destroy (gameObject);
    }
}
```

Note that in the `Update()` function, `Time.deltaTime * 5` is added behind the movement equation. `Time.deltaTime` is basically the time passed in each tick/frame. By multiplying the direction vector with the delta time, the movement becomes frame rate independent and the movement speed is guaranteed to be consistent across different computers. The number 5 behind the delta time is the speed of the movement. You can increase the number to make the movement faster or decrease it to make it slower.

After this, open up `PlayerAttack` script that we created in the previous chapter. Declare a variable named `bulletPrefab` at the beginning of the `PlayerAttack` class:

```
    public GameObject bulletPrefab;
```

Then, add the following code to the bottom of the `Update()` function:

```
    if (Input.GetMouseButtonDown(1))
    {
        if (playerAttr.manaPoint >= 100)
        {


            for (int i = 0; i < 8; ++i)
    {
        Instantiate(bulletPrefab, transform.position +
        new Vector3(0, 1, 0), transform.rotation * Quaternion.Euler(new
        Vector3(0, 45 * i, 0)));
    }

            playerAttr.manaPoint -= 100;
        }
    }
```

The preceding code will check whether the player's mana point is 100 (full mana). If it does, then it will spawn eight bullets at the player's position, each having a 45 degree increment in its rotation value. After spawning the bullet prefabs, we will decrease the mana point and make it empty.

This is how it looks in action:

After you have triggered the special attack for the first time, try to trigger it again, and this time nothing happens. This is because the mana point is not 100, and thus you need to go and get the power-up to restore the mana point before you can use the special attack again.

Improving enemy AI

In the previous chapter, we learned how to create enemies that will chase the player if too close with it. However, the enemies look very stiff because they don't move at all when the player is not within its sight. Therefore, we will adjust the AI script a little bit to make the enemies able to patrol around the level randomly if the player is not detected.

First of all, open up the EnemyAI script and add these variables on top:

```
Vector3 randomPos;
float pauseInterval = 0;
float pauseTime = 0;
```

The randomPos variable is where the enemy will be moving to during patrolling. The randomPos variable will be recalculated if the enemy has reached that position. The enemy will stand still for a while before moving to the next random position.

Next, add `CalculateRandomPosition()` to the `Start()` function:

```
void Start ()
{
  // Find player
  player = GameObject.FindWithTag ("Player");
  CalculateRandomPosition ();
}
```

This is how the `CalculateRandomPosition()` function looks:

```
void CalculateRandomPosition ()
{
  NavMeshHit hit;
  NavMesh.SamplePosition (transform.position + Random.
  insideUnitSphere * Random.Range(3, 10), out hit, 10,
  NavMesh.AllAreas);

  randomPos = hit.position;
}
```

Basically, what `CalculateRandomPosition()` does is randomly pick a position around a given range from the enemy's current position.

After this, replace the entire `Update()` function with the following code:

```
void Update ()
{
  if (player != null)
  {
    // Check if player is nearby
    if (Vector3.Distance(transform.position,
    player.transform.position) < 6)
    {
      // Move toward player
      agent.SetDestination(player.transform.position);
    }
    else
    {
      // If reached the nearby random position
      if (Vector3.Distance(transform.position, randomPos) < 3)
      {
        // Recalculate nearby random position
        CalculateRandomPosition();
```

```
        // Calculate the time to start moving again
        pauseInterval = Random.Range(2, 10);
        pauseTime = Time.time + pauseInterval;
    }
    else
    {
        // Already passed the pausing interval
        if (pauseTime < Time.time)
        {
            // Move to random nearby location
            agent.SetDestination(randomPos);

            // Just in-case if the AI stuck,
            recalculate random point
            if (agent.velocity == Vector3.zero)
            {
                CalculateRandomPosition();
            }
        }
    }
}
    }
}
```

Adding save points

We want to allow the player to save his/her game progression and continue playing the game in some other days. Some games allow the player to save the game anytime, but some require the player to reach the save point in order to do so. For the first option, you'll need to save a lot more data, especially if the game is action-heavy and not turn-based; otherwise, problems may occur. This is because an action-heavy genre, such as action RPG and FPS, has so many events happening at the same time that if you don't save the current states of all the AIs, events, movements, physics, and so on, the game will not be correctly restored when the player tries to load back the saved game next time.

With the save point, problems like this can be avoided because the game designer will make sure that the save point is being placed at a place where player is certainly safe and no important game event is going on in that area at that time; therefore, less data is needed to be saved.

Here, I made a save point prefab using several cubes and parented the cube to an empty object. Then, I applied a sphere collider to it and ticked the **is trigger** option.

After this, I also created a dialog user interface for player to confirm whether to save the game, as shown in the following screenshot:

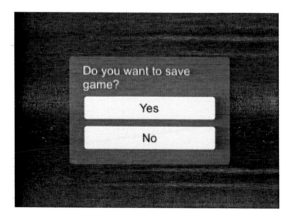

Then, we will create two C# scripts, one called `SavePoint.cs` and another called `SaveManager.cs`. Basically, the `SavePoint` script will trigger the **save** dialog, whereas the `SaveManager` script will handle the game saving mechanism.

`SavePoint.cs` is very simple; it will detect if an enemy has collided with the player and ask the `saveManager` object to show the **save** dialog user interface if it does. Here's the script for `SavePoint.cs`:

```
using UnityEngine;
using System.Collections;

public class SavePoint : MonoBehaviour
{
  public SaveManager saveManager;

  void OnTriggerEnter (Collider col)
  {
    if (col.tag == "Player")
    {
      saveManager.ShowSaveDialogUI ();
    }
  }
}
```

`SaveManager.cs`, however, is much more complicated. The script is divided into two parts: the first part consists of functions related to the **save** dialog user interface and the second part is where the game saving code is written. Here is the first part of the script, which consists of two functions: `ShowSaveDialogUI ()` and `HideSaveDialogUI ()`, which are both self-explanatory by their names:

```
public GameObject saveDialogUI;

void Start ()
{
  HideSaveDialogUI ();
}

public void ShowSaveDialogUI ()
{
  saveDialogUI.SetActive (true);

  // Stop time and unhide cursor
  Time.timeScale = 0;
```

```
      Cursor.lockState = CursorLockMode.None;
      Cursor.visible = true;
   }

   public void HideSaveDialogUI ()
   {
      saveDialogUI.SetActive (false);

      // Continue time and hide cursor
      Time.timeScale = 1;
      Cursor.lockState = CursorLockMode.Locked;
      Cursor.visible = false;
   }
```

After this, we will dive into the `SaveGame()` function, which handles the game saving mechanism. `PlayerPrefs` is a class in the Unity API that handles data saving. You can save a value by using `SaveFloat()`, `SaveInt()`, or `SaveString()`, and then you can load it back by calling `GetFloat()`, `GetInt()`, or `GetString()`.

> For more information regarding `PlayerPrefs`, do check out the Scripting API documentation at `http://docs.unity3d.com/ScriptReference/PlayerPrefs.html`.

First thing we need to do is clear all the previously saved data using `PlayerPrefs.DeleteAll()` so that we don't overlap some of the old data that no longer exists in the current state. For example, the player has saved the game in level A, but has continued to level B and is trying to save the data in the second level. This will cause the data of level B to be overlapped with the data of level A and may cause a lot of trouble when loading back the game. To make sure that no such problem occurs in our game, delete everything before saving the new data.

After this, we will save the current level name so that we know which level to load when we click on **Continue Game** from the main menu. Then, we will proceed with saving the player's data. There are few things that we need to save here—the position and rotation of the player character and its attributes, including level, health point, mana point, and so on. After this, we also need to save the player camera's position and rotation so that when the game is loaded, the camera view is at the correct location.

Then, we will save the enemies' data. For this one, we will need to find all the enemies in the scene with the `Monster` tag by calling `GameObject.FindGameObjects WithTag("Monster")` and loop through all the resulting game objects to save data of each enemy. To distinguish between each enemy, we will save its instance ID set by Unity, which is guaranteed to be unique, by calling `gameObject.GetInstanceID()`. When the saved game is loaded back, we will match the instance ID of all the enemies with the saved data to correctly restore the states of the enemies. We are not only saving the position, rotation, and health point of the enemies, but also an *alive* state, which determines whether the enemy has been defeated or not. If it's already defeated, it will be deleted when the saved game is being loaded.

Last but not least, we will save the data of all the items in the scene. The same method is being used for the items, that is, find all the items in the scene with the `Item` tag, loop through the resulting game objects, and save its *exist* state. If the item has already been taken by the player, it will no longer exist, and thus the *exist* state will not be saved. Items that have no *exist* state will be removed when the saved game is being loaded.

The full code of `SaveGame()` function is shown here:

```
public void SaveGame ()
{
  // Clear everything
  PlayerPrefs.DeleteAll ();

  // Save game level data
  PlayerPrefs.SetString ("level_name",
  Application.loadedLevelName);

  // Save player data
  GameObject player = GameObject.FindWithTag ("Player");

  PlayerPrefs.SetFloat ("player_posX",
  player.transform.position.x);
  PlayerPrefs.SetFloat ("player_posY",
  player.transform.position.y);
  PlayerPrefs.SetFloat ("player_posZ",
  player.transform.position.z);

  PlayerPrefs.SetFloat ("player_rotX",
  player.transform.rotation.x);
  PlayerPrefs.SetFloat ("player_rotY",
  player.transform.rotation.y);
```

```
PlayerPrefs.SetFloat ("player_rotZ",
player.transform.rotation.z);

PlayerStat playerStat = player.GetComponent<PlayerStat>();

PlayerPrefs.SetFloat ("player_level", playerStat.level);
PlayerPrefs.SetFloat ("player_healthPoint",
playerStat.healthPoint);
PlayerPrefs.SetFloat ("player_manaPoint", playerStat.manaPoint);
PlayerPrefs.SetFloat ("player_attackDamage",
playerStat.attackDamage);
PlayerPrefs.SetFloat ("player_specialAttackDamage",
playerStat.specialAttackDamage);
PlayerPrefs.SetFloat ("player_defense", playerStat.defense);

// Save player camera data
GameObject gameCamera = GameObject.FindWithTag ("Camera");

PlayerPrefs.SetFloat ("camera_posX",
gameCamera.transform.position.x);
PlayerPrefs.SetFloat ("camera_posY",
gameCamera.transform.position.y);
PlayerPrefs.SetFloat ("camera_posZ",
gameCamera.transform.position.z);

PlayerPrefs.SetFloat ("camera_rotX",
gameCamera.transform.rotation.x);
PlayerPrefs.SetFloat ("camera_rotY",
gameCamera.transform.rotation.y);
PlayerPrefs.SetFloat ("camera_rotZ",
gameCamera.transform.rotation.z);

// Save monsters data
GameObject[] allMonsters = GameObject.
FindGameObjectsWithTag ("Monster");
foreach (GameObject monster in allMonsters)
{
  PlayerPrefs.SetInt("monster" + monster.GetInstanceID()
  + "_alive", 1);

  PlayerPrefs.SetFloat ("monster" + monster.GetInstanceID()
  + "_posX", monster.transform.position.x);
  PlayerPrefs.SetFloat ("monster" + monster.GetInstanceID()
  + "_posY", monster.transform.position.y);
```

```
        PlayerPrefs.SetFloat ("monster" + monster.GetInstanceID()
        + "_posZ", monster.transform.position.z);

        PlayerPrefs.SetFloat ("monster" + monster.GetInstanceID()
        + "_rotX", monster.transform.rotation.x);
        PlayerPrefs.SetFloat ("monster" + monster.GetInstanceID()
        + "_rotX", monster.transform.rotation.y);
        PlayerPrefs.SetFloat ("monster" + monster.GetInstanceID()
        + "_rotX", monster.transform.rotation.z);

        EnemyAI enemyStat = monster.GetComponent<EnemyAI>();

        PlayerPrefs.SetFloat ("monster" + monster.GetInstanceID()
        + "_healthPoint", enemyStat.healthPoint);
    }

    // Save item data
    GameObject[] allItems = GameObject.FindGameObjectsWithTag
    ("Item");
    foreach (GameObject item in allItems)
    {
        PlayerPrefs.SetInt("item" + item.GetInstanceID() +
        "_exist", 1);
    }

    HideSaveDialogUI ();
}
```

 Unity's `PlayerPrefs` class saves all the data unencrypted. If data security is critical for your game project, you can search for encrypted `PlayerPrefs` in the Unity Asset Store.

Next, we will write the LoadGame() function used to restore the saved data. It's basically very similar to the preceding SaveGame() function; the only difference is that instead of SetFloat() and SetInt(), we use GetFloat and GetInt() to retrieve data from the disk. Here's the code for the LoadGame() function:

```
public void LoadGame ()
{
    // Load player data
    GameObject player = GameObject.FindWithTag ("Player");

    Vector3 playerPos = new Vector3 ();
    playerPos.x = PlayerPrefs.GetFloat ("player_posX", 0);
    playerPos.y = PlayerPrefs.GetFloat ("player_posY", 0);
```

```
playerPos.z = PlayerPrefs.GetFloat ("player_posZ", 0);
player.transform.position = playerPos;

Quaternion playerRot = new Quaternion ();
playerRot.x = PlayerPrefs.GetFloat ("player_rotX", 0);
playerRot.y = PlayerPrefs.GetFloat ("player_rotY", 0);
playerRot.z = PlayerPrefs.GetFloat ("player_rotZ", 0);
player.transform.rotation = playerRot;

PlayerStat playerStat = player.GetComponent<PlayerStat>();

playerStat.level = PlayerPrefs.GetInt ("player_level", 0);
playerStat.healthPoint = PlayerPrefs.GetFloat
("player_healthPoint", 0);
playerStat.manaPoint = PlayerPrefs.GetFloat
("player_manaPoint", 0);
playerStat.attackDamage = PlayerPrefs.GetFloat
("player_attackDamage", 0);
playerStat.specialAttackDamage = PlayerPrefs.GetFloat
("player_specialAttackDamage", 0);
playerStat.defense = PlayerPrefs.GetFloat ("player_defense", 0);

// Load player camera data
GameObject gameCamera = GameObject.FindWithTag ("Camera");

Vector3 cameraPos = new Vector3 ();
cameraPos.x = PlayerPrefs.GetFloat ("camera_posX", 0);
cameraPos.y = PlayerPrefs.GetFloat ("camera_posY", 0);
cameraPos.z = PlayerPrefs.GetFloat ("camera_posZ", 0);
gameCamera.transform.position = cameraPos;

Quaternion cameraRot = new Quaternion ();
cameraRot.x = PlayerPrefs.GetFloat ("camera_rotX", 0);
cameraRot.y = PlayerPrefs.GetFloat ("camera_rotY", 0);
cameraRot.z = PlayerPrefs.GetFloat ("camera_rotZ", 0);
gameCamera.transform.rotation = cameraRot;

// Load monsters data
GameObject[] allMonsters = GameObject.FindGameObjectsWithTag
("Monster");
foreach (GameObject monster in allMonsters)
{
  // Check if monster already defeated previously
  if (PlayerPrefs.GetInt("monster" + monster.GetInstanceID()
  + "_alive", 0) == 0)
```

```
      {
        // Monster died
        Destroy(monster);
      }
      else
      {
        Vector3 monsterPos = new Vector3 ();
        monsterPos.x = PlayerPrefs.GetFloat ("monster" +
        monster.GetInstanceID() + "_posX", 0);
        monsterPos.y = PlayerPrefs.GetFloat ("monster" +
        monster.GetInstanceID() + "_posY", 0);
        monsterPos.z = PlayerPrefs.GetFloat ("monster" +
        monster.GetInstanceID() + "_posZ", 0);
        monster.transform.position = monsterPos;

        Quaternion monsterRot = new Quaternion ();
        monsterRot.x = PlayerPrefs.GetFloat ("monster" +
        monster.GetInstanceID() + "_rotX", 0);
        monsterRot.y = PlayerPrefs.GetFloat ("monster" +
        monster.GetInstanceID() + "_rotX", 0);
        monsterRot.z = PlayerPrefs.GetFloat ("monster" +
        monster.GetInstanceID() + "_rotX", 0);
        monster.transform.rotation = monsterRot;

        EnemyAI enemyStat = monster.GetComponent<EnemyAI>();

        enemyStat.healthPoint = PlayerPrefs.GetFloat ("monster"
        + monster.GetInstanceID() + "_healthPoint", 0);
      }
    }

    // Load item data
    GameObject[] allItems = GameObject.FindGameObjectsWithTag
    ("Item");
    foreach (GameObject item in allItems)
    {
      if (PlayerPrefs.GetInt("item" + item.GetInstanceID() +
      "_exist", 0) == 0)
      {
        Destroy (item);
      }
    }
  }
}
```

With the preceding code, we get the following output:

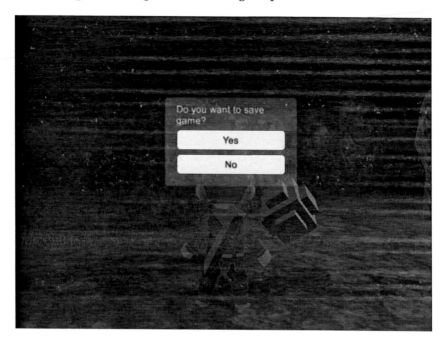

Summary

In this chapter, you learned how to create player attributes and change its values through in-game items and power-ups, as well as to utilize the attributes for special attacks. You also learned how to create much more sophisticated enemies that patrol around the game level if player is not within its line of sight. Finally, you also learned how to save the game progression as well as being able to restore it correctly anytime you want.

In the next chapter, we will walk you through on how to improve the visual aesthetics using screen effects and particles!

8
Post-Production and Visual FX

In this chapter, we will learn how to enhance our game's visual appearance by using particles and image effects.

In this chapter, we will cover:

- A basic particle system
- Mist particles
- Torch fire
- Image FX
- Quality settings

A basic particle system

Particle systems are often overlooked by rookie game developers because they are not something that will affect game mechanics, or make the AI smarter. However, a particle system is very important in games because not only does it make a static and boring scene look a lot livelier, but it can also create different moods and affect the player's emotion. Particles can be applied to game environments, props, power-ups, weapons, magic skills, and so on.

To create a particle system, go to **Create | Particle System**, and it will create an empty object with the particle system attached to it. The particle system in Unity is in the form of a component and it has to be attached onto a game object in order for it to be functional, which means you can add the particle system to any game object, not necessarily an empty object only. Then, you will see something like this:

When a particle system is selected, a small window will appear at the bottom-right corner of your 3D scene. You can use this window to play, pause, or stop the particle system for testing purposes. You can also adjust the playback speed and playback time when testing the particles.

Next, you will also see a bunch of settings appearing on the **Inspector** window. Don't worry, as we will go through the settings one by one.

- **The Main module**: This contains the global properties of the particle, such as duration, looped, start size, start color, gravity multiplier, and so on. Unlike all the other modules, this module cannot be disabled.

- **Emission**: The **Emission** module controls the rate and timing of particle emissions.

- **Shape**: This module is used to select the shape of the emission volume where particles are spawned from within it. The types of shapes include sphere, hemisphere, cone, box, mesh, circle, and edge.

- **Velocity over Lifetime**: You can set this to increase or decrease the velocity of the particles over their lifetime, relative to either the local space or the world space.

- **Limit Velocity over Lifetime**: This module controls how the speed of particles is reduced over their lifetime.

- **Force over Lifetime**: You can add additional forces to the particles to simulate wind, attraction, and so on. You can also select whether the force has been applied in the local space or world space.

- **Color over Lifetime**: This module controls the color of particles over time.
- **Color by Speed**: This module changes the color of the particles according to its speed in distance units per second.
- **Size over Lifetime**: You can make the particles expand or shrink over time using this module.
- **Size by Speed**: The size of a particle can be set here to change according to its speed in distance units per second.
- **Rotation over Lifetime**: You can make your particles look more realistic by assigning an angular velocity to them as they move.
- **Rotation by Speed**: The rotation of a particle can be set here to change according to its speed in distance units per second.
- **External Forces**: By enabling this module, your particles will be affected by the wind zones in your game scene. The higher the value you set for the multiplier property, the stronger it will be affected by the wind zones.
- **Collision**: This controls the way particles collide with solid objects in the scene.
- **Sub Emitters**: If you want to spawn additional particle systems at certain stages of its lifetime, you can enable this module. Phases of the particle's life include birth, collision, and death.
- **Texture Sheet Animation**: You can animate your particles' texture by using this module. All you need to do is provide a texture with image sequence fits in grids, and then set the properties of this module to let it know how many rows there are in total and how many frames of animation there are to play as time progresses.
- **Renderer**: This module's settings determine how a particle's image or mesh is transformed, shaded, and overdrawn by other particles. You can also change the material of the particle here.

After we have learned all the modules within a particle system, it's time for us to make use of them. Let's try to create a simple particle effect that gets spawned when the player has obtained an item or power-up.

First, change the settings in the Main module, as follows:

- **Duration**: 0.5
- **Start Lifetime**: 0.4
- **Start Speed**: 8
- **Start Size**: 0.5
- **Max Particle**: 1000

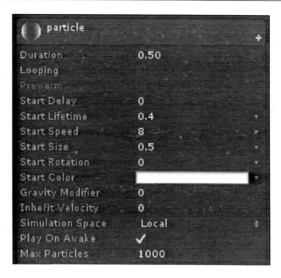

Then, change the emission rate to 50. After that, change the emitter shape from cone to sphere, and keep the radius as 1. Then, enable **Size over Lifetime** and click on the little box besides the **Size** setting. Make sure that the line in the box turns red after you've clicked on it. After that, scroll up a little bit until you see the **Open Editor** button in the **Inspector** window. Click on it to open up the particle graph editor, which looks something like this:

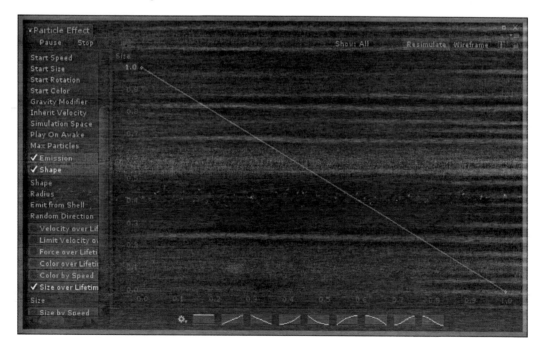

Change the graph under **Size over Lifetime** into a slanted line, as you can see in the preceding screenshot. This means the particle's size will decrease from the start size (0 in this case) to zero overtime.

Once you're done with all the settings, let's create a new C# script called ItemParticles.cs. The script is very simple; what it does is destroy the particle after two seconds:

```
using UnityEngine;
using System.Collections;

public class ItemParticles : MonoBehaviour
{
  void Start()
  {
    StartCoroutine (DestroyParticles());
  }

  IEnumerator DestroyParticles()
  {
    yield return new WaitForSeconds(2);
    Destroy (gameObject);
  }
}
```

Apply the script to your particle game object and save it as a prefab. Then, we will change the PowerUp.cs script so that it will spawn the particle when the player is colliding with it. We only have to add two new lines of code to the PowerUp script, as shown in the following highlight:

```
using UnityEngine;
using System.Collections;

public class PowerUp : MonoBehaviour
{
  public float addHealthPoint = 0;
  public float addManaPoint = 0;
  public float addAttackDamage = 0;
  public float addSpecialAttackDamage = 0;
  public float addDefense = 0;

  public GameObject particlePrefab;

  void OnTriggerEnter (Collider col)
```

```
    {
      if (col.gameObject.CompareTag("Player"))
      {
        PlayerAttribute playeAttr =
        col.gameObject.GetComponent<PlayerAttribute>();
        playeAttr.manaPoint += addManaPoint;
        playeAttr.healthPoint += addHealthPoint;
        playeAttr.attackDamage += addAttackDamage;
        playeAttr.specialAttackDamage += addSpecialAttackDamage;
        playeAttr.defense += addDefense;

        Instantiate(particlePrefab, transform.position,
        transform.rotation);

        Destroy(gameObject);
      }
    }
  }
```

Lastly, link the particle prefab to all the powerup prefabs so that it will work properly. Here's the final result:

Mist particles

Next, we will learn how to add some spooky and mysterious atmospherics to our game scene by creating a mist particle system. Start by creating an empty game object, then apply a particle system component to it. Because our scene is so huge, we'll need to make the particle system cover the entire scene. To achieve that, change the shape of the emitter to **Box**, and change its scale until it covers the entire scene. After that, check the **Random Direction** option so that particles will be spawned facing a random direction. That will make the mist look more natural.

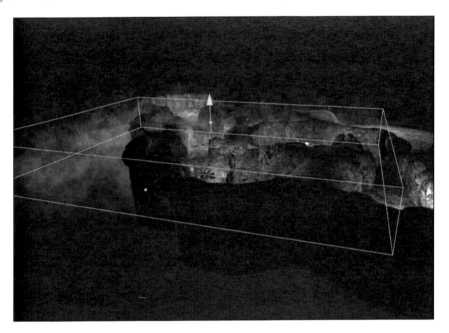

Then, we will adjust the settings in the Main module:

- **Duration**: 100
- **Looping**: Enable
- **Prewarm**: Enable
- **Start Lifetime**: 100
- **Start Speed**: 0.1
- **Start Size**: 1
- **Start Color**: A gradient of total transparency to opaque white

- **Max Particle**: 10000

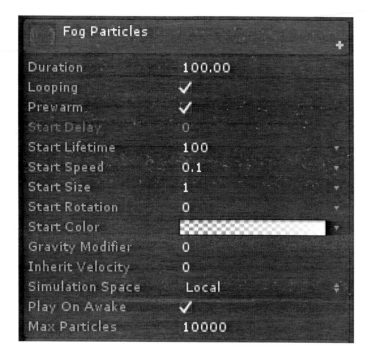

The start color looks something like this in the gradient editor:

We want the particles to be totally transparent when it gets spawned, and gradually change to opaque. After that, set the emission rate to 10 and enable the **Color over Lifetime** module. Set the color to the reverse order from the start color because we want the particles to slowly fade out over time. Then, enable **Rotation over Lifetime** and change **Constant** to **Random between Two Constants**. Set the values to -5 and 5, just to give the particles a little bit of random rotation to make the mist look more natural.

After we're done with the particle settings, we will move on to create the material for the mist particles. Use a texture that has a black color background:

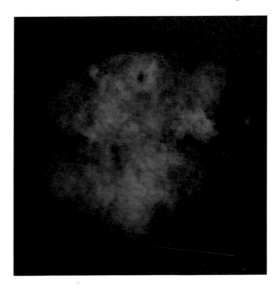

The black color will be converted to transparency by selecting the texture and checking both **Alpha from Grayscale** and **Alpha is Transparency** on the **Inspector** window. Next, create a new material, change the shader type to **Particles/Additive (Soft)**, and apply the texture to it. Finally, replace the default material in the **Renderer** module of the mist particle system with the new material that you just created.

The mist particles in action:

Torch fire

Next, we will learn how to create a more sophisticated particle by using a texture sheet. For this example, we will be creating a torch and a particle system that will be used as the torch fire. Again, we will create an empty game object and apply a new particle system to it. Then, we will set the settings in the Main module:

- **Duration**: 1
- **Looping**: Enable
- **Start Lifetime**: 1
- **Start Speed**: 0
- **Start Size**: 2

- **Max Particles**: 1

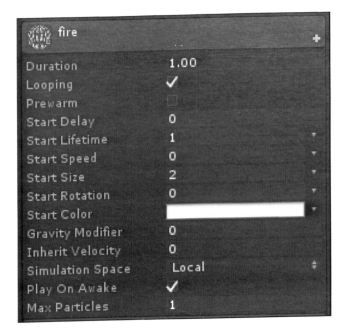

Then, set the emission rate to 1. In this case, we only need one single particle to be spawned by the particle system and kept alive until the animation has finished playing.

Next, we will create a new material and apply the following texture to the material:

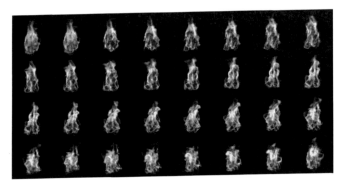

After that, let's get back to the particle system again, and set the shader type of the material to **Particles/Additive**. After that, enable the **Texture Sheet Animation** module and set the **Tiles** setting to:

- **X**: 8

- **Y**: 4

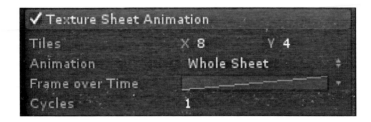

You can easily get this number by looking at how many columns and rows of frames there are on the texture. Then, apply the material to your particle system at the **Renderer** module. Create a cylinder, scale it, and apply the fire particle on top of it to emulate a torch.

The end result looks like this:

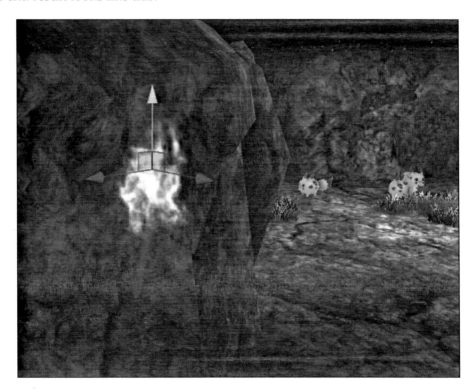

Image FX

Normally, in the post-production stage of a live-action film or an animation, video editors will start adjusting the visuals of the video footage before compiling it into the final video. Tons of effects will be applied to the footage and the overall color and mood will be carefully adjusted to fit the style they want. This process is what we call **compositing**.

In video games, a similar process exists at the end of production to enhance the visual quality, as well as to create the intended mood. In Unity, there is no built-in system for you to do this. However, you can download the free Standard Assets pack provided by Unity Technologies at the Unity Asset Store. This package includes image effect scripts that we will be using to enhance our game's visuals.

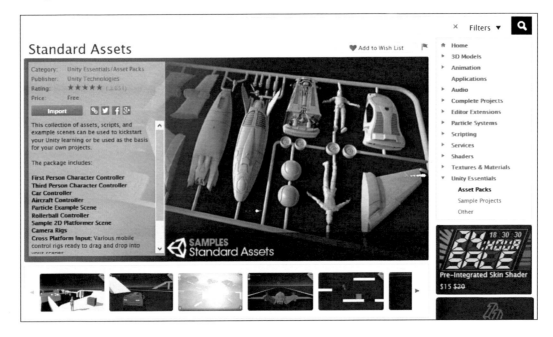

After you have downloaded the Standard Assets package, import it to your Unity project. The package is mixed with some other things that we don't need at the moment, so we will just enable the `Editor` folder and the `Effects` folder. Then, click on the **Import** button to start importing.

Once you have imported the package to your project, you can now apply the image effects to your game camera by going to **Component | Image Effects**. There are numerous amounts of image effects that you can find in the **Image Effects** menu, which is divided into several different categories:

- **Bloom and Glow**: This category includes screen effects such as bloom and lens flares. Bloom is the optical effect where light from a bright source appears to leak into surrounding objects. It can be used to achieve both a dream-like visual or to enhance realism, depending on how much bloom effect you set to your camera. There are several different types of bloom effects in this category, and one of them also generates anamorphic lens flares to help evoke a cinematic feeling.

- **Blur**: The second category consists of screen effects that cause the screen to become blurry. The blur script simply allows you to blur the entire screen, and the motion blur script simulates motion trails when a camera moves.

- **Camera**: The **Camera** category contains several screen effects such as camera motion blur, depth of field, tilt shift, vignette, and chromatic aberration. The camera motion blur is an enhancement to the motion blur script in the previous category. This modern approach to motion blur keeps track of every moving object and generates a velocity buffer in order to apply different levels of blurriness to different areas of the screen based on the movement speed of each object, as well as its depth in relation to the camera. The depth of field script simulates the properties of a camera lens by focusing sharply on an object at a specific distance and blurring out other areas that are not in focus. Similarly, the tilt shift effect blurs the screen based on the distance to the center, instead of focusing on a certain object in the distance. Lastly, vignette and chromatic aberration introduce darkening, blur, and spectral color separation at the edges and corners of the screen to simulate a view through the camera lens, but can also be used to create abstract effects.

- **Color Adjustments**: This category consists of scripts that change the color of the rendered image onscreen. The color correction scripts make adjustments to the hue, saturation, brightness, and contrast of the screen using different methods, such as using color correction curves, ramp texture, or lookup texture. The contrast enhancement script, on the other hand, only changes the contrast of the screen according to the intensity value that you set. Other than that, the gray scale and sepia tone scripts are both used to remap the screen colors to a single set of hue, making the visuals resemble an old photograph. Lastly, the tone mapping script is the process of mapping color values from **HDR (high dynamic range)** to **LDR (low dynamic range)**. This enables interesting dynamic effects, such as a simulation of the natural adaption that happens when entering or leaving a dark tunnel into bright sunlight. Note that tone mapping will only work properly if the used camera is HDR enabled.

- **Edge Detection**: Both the crease shading and edge detection scripts contained in this category are common **non-photorealistic rendering (NPR)** techniques that enhance the visibility of objects by adding outlines or black edges of variable thickness.

- **Displacement**: This contains screen effects that cause distortion to the rendered image, such as fish eye, twirl, and vortex effects.

- **Rendering**: Screen effect scripts such as global fog, screen space ambient occlusion, screen space ambient obscurance, and sun shaft can be found in this category. Global fog, as its name implies, simulates a camera-based exponential fog effect based on world space calculation. Screen space ambient occlusion is an image effect that darkens creases, holes, and surfaces that are close to each other, imitating a real-life scenario where such areas tend to block out or occlude ambient light, and hence they appear darker. Screen space ambient obscurance, on the other hand, is an improvement to the screen space ambient occlusion in terms of quality and speed. Instead of relying on a generated normals buffer, it creates the effect on the fly based on depth. Other than that, this category also contains the sun shaft effect script. Sun shaft (also known as **cloud ray** or **god ray**) is an image effect that simulates the radial light scattering that arises when a very bright light source is partly obscured.

- **Noise**: This consists of camera effects such as noise, grain, and scratches that simulate noise and film grain, which is a typical effect that happens in film, photography, or TV/VCR.

- **Other**: This contains two scripts: antialiasing and screen overlay. Antialiasing as a post-processing effect offers a set of algorithms designed to give a smoother appearance to graphics. When two areas of different colors adjoin in an image, the shape of the pixels can form a very distinctive *staircase* along the boundary. This effect is known as **aliasing**, and hence antialiasing refers to any measure that reduces the effect. There are several different types of antialiasing that you can choose from the script, such as SSAA, NFAA, FXAA II, FXAA III, DLAA, and so on. Each algorithm produces a slightly different result and varies in performance. The screen overlay script, on the other hand, introduces an easy way to blend different kinds of textures over the entire screen to create custom looks or effects.

It's very easy to apply these effects to your game. All you need to do is add the image effect script to your active game camera and you're done! You can also apply several scripts to the camera at the same time, but do notice that the more effects you have applied to your game camera, the more computational power is needed to generate these effects, which may not work on older computers or mobile phones.

The following is the result of adding screen space ambient occlusion, bloom, and depth of field effects to my camera; pretty neat!

Quality settings

Last but not least, it's also very important to set the quality settings for our game in order to balance visual quality and performance. Unity allows us to pick a different set of quality settings for different platforms. You can open up the **QualitySettings** window by going to **Edit | Project Settings | Quality**.

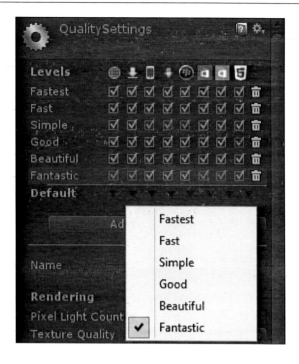

As you can see, all the mobile platforms have been set to the **Simple** quality level compared to the rest, which are set to **Fantastic** or **Good**. You can change the default quality level of each platform by clicking on the small arrow below the quality levels. You can still change the quality level inside the game provided that you have a quality settings UI for the players to do so.

Each quality level contains a set of settings that affect how Unity handles the rendering process. The settings include:

- **Pixel Light Count**: The maximum number of pixel lights when forward rendering is used.

- **Texture Quality**: This allows you to choose the maximum resolution of the textures used in your game. The options are **Full Res**, **Half Res**, **Quarter Res**, and **Eighth Res**.

- **Anisotropic Textures**: This enables if and how anisotropic textures will be used. The options are **Disabled**, **Per Texture**, and **Forced On**.

- **Antialiasing**: This sets the level of antialiasing that will be used. This antialiasing is different from the antialiasing effect script that we learned in the previous section. Instead of applying an effect to the rendered image, this **Antialiasing** setting simply tells the Unity renderer to render the image several times larger than the window screen, then scale it back to the screen size again to reduce the *staircase* effect. This technique is what we call **multi-sampling**. The options for the antialiasing are 2x, 4x, and 8x multi-sampling.

- **Soft Particles**: This is set if soft blending should be used for particles.

- **Real-time Reflection Probes**: This is set if reflection probes should be updated during gameplay.

- **Billboard Face Camera Position**: This is set if the billboards face toward the camera position or face toward the camera plane.

- **Shadows**: This determines which type of shadows should be used. The available options are **Hard and Soft Shadows**, **Hard Shadows Only**, and **Disable Shadows**.

- **Shadow Resolution**: This sets the resolution of the shadow. Options are **Low**, **Medium**, **High**, and **Very High**. The higher the resolution, the greater the processing overhead will be.

- **Shadow Projection**: This setting is used to determine the method used for shadow projection. There are two different options for this. The first one is called **Close Fit**, which renders the shadow at a higher resolution but may cause a wobble effect when the camera moves. The second option is called **Stable Fit**, which renders lower-resolution shadows but they don't wobble with camera movements.

- **Shadow Distance**: This indicates the maximum distance from the camera at which shadows will be visible. Shadows that fall beyond this distance will not be rendered.

- **Shadow Cascades**: A higher number of cascades gives a better-quality shadow but at the expense of processing overhead. The options for this are zero, two, and four. You can also set how the cascades are being split.

- **Blend Weights**: This indicates the number of bones that can affect a given vertex during an animation. The available options are one, two, or four bones.

- **V Sync Count**: Set the **V Sync Count** setting to enable synchronization of the rendering with the display device's refresh rate to avoid *tearing* artifacts.

- **LOD Bias**: The **LOD (level of details)** levels are chosen based on the onscreen size of an object. When the size is between two LOD levels, the choice can be biased toward the less detailed or more detailed of the two models available.

- **Maximum LOD Level**: This setting is used to determine the highest LOD that will be used by the game.

- **Particle Ray cast Budget**: The maximum number of ray casts to use for approximate particle system collisions can be set here.

Most of the time, the default settings work just fine. However, if you want more control on how your game should work, Unity provides you with all these options to do just that!

Summary

In this chapter, you have learned how to enhance the visual of your game by creating particle effects and applying image effects to the game camera. You have also learned how to adjust the quality settings for your game so that you don't sacrifice performance for good visuals.

In the next chapter, we will walk you through how to deploy your game!

9
Deploying the Game

In this chapter, we will learn how to configure our game's settings, such as window title, icon, rendering settings, and so on before deploying the game to a chosen platform.

In this chapter, we will cover:

- Build settings
- Player settings

Build settings

Deploying a game in Unity is quite straightforward; if you have already set the build settings and built the game before, just go to **File | Build & Run** to straightaway build it again without changing the settings. If you have not built the game before and have clicked on **Build & Run**, Unity will automatically open up the **Build Settings** window for you, which you can also access by going to **File | Build Settings**.

The **Build Settings** window looks like so:

As you can see from the window, the settings are minimal and could be different depending on which target platform you're selecting. You can try to choose a different platform, then click on the **Switch Platform** button to make the switch. It may take some time for Unity to automatically convert all the game assets into formats that are compatible with the selected platform, and no action is required on your side. However, some target platforms are not available in the free version of Unity; check out Unity's official website to find out more about this.

On the lower-right of the **Build Settings** window, you will see several different options, such as target platform, architecture, development build, and so on. Again, it varies depending on the platform you've chosen. Next I have listed the settings for some of the more popular platforms, such as Web Player, PC, iOS, Android, and WebGL, and I will explain to you what each of these settings mean.

Shared settings

Shared settings is where you define various parameters that are shared across different target platforms.

- **Development Build**: If this option is checked, Unity will display debugging information in your game, such as outlines and logs, for easy debugging. Unity will also include debugging symbols and enable the ability to connect to the profiler.

- **Autoconnect Profiler**: This only becomes active if you checked **Development Build**. It will allow Unity to automatically pick up an active profiler during debugging.

- **Script Debugging**: This option will allow Unity to inspect your code at runtime. It can help you determine when a function is called and with which values. Unity uses MonoDevelop to debug the scripts in your game, so make sure that MonoDevelop is installed on your computer.

The webplayer

The webplayer is in an odd state at the time of writing this book. Due to the discontinued support of NPAPI in the latest versions of Chrome, Unity web player no longer work on the Chrome browser. Moreover, other web browsers will likely follow suit, which means if there is no alternative to NPAPI, Unity web player will most likely become obsolete in the near future.

- **Streamed**: Instead of waiting for all the contents of the game level to be downloaded before allowing the player to start playing your game, this option allows the game to start running while downloading the contents at the same time. However, this requires a lot of tuning and structuring to your game so that it can seamlessly run and load without the player noticing it.

- **Offline Deployment**: By checking this option, Unity will place the UnityObject.js file, which is used to interface the player with the host page, alongside the web player during the build. This enables the player to work with the local script file even when there is no network connection.

PC, Mac, and Linux standalone

Here, you can set the build settings for all the three major desktop operating systems: Windows, Mac OS X, and Linux.

- **Target Platform**: You can choose between Windows, Mac OS X, or Linux as the target platform for deployment.
- **Architecture**: For Windows, you can choose between x86 (32 bit) or x86_64 (64 bit). For Mac OS X and Linux, you can choose between x86, x86_64, or Universal build (32 bit + 64 bit).

iOS

This section provides an extra option specifically for the iOS platform.

- **Symlink Unity Libraries**: **Symlink Unity Libraries** creates a link to the original core libraries that have already been built on the Unity side of the project when generating an iOS Xcode project for faster iteration time and smaller build folders.

Android

This is where you change the build settings for the Android platform.

- **Texture Compression**: By default, Unity uses the ETC1/RGBA16 format for all the textures used in the game. If you wish to build your game for a specific hardware architecture, you can override this default behavior by choosing a different format from the drop-down box. This option is designed for advanced users.
- **Google Android Project**: By checking this option, Unity generates a project that can be opened by Android Studio, instead of directly generating an APK file and exporting it to the device.

WebGL

WebGL is a relatively new platform compared to the others. It is still not very stable at the time of writing this book; however, it may become the "de facto" web platform in Unity if the web player is to be deprecated in the near future.

Optimization level

This option allows you to select an optimization flag for the compiler that builds your game. When set to **Slow**, Unity produces an unoptimized build that is bigger in size and causes slower performance but is much faster to build. This allows you to quickly test your game and iterate on code issues. The **Fast** option produces optimized builds, and **Fastest** enables some additional optimizations, but makes your builds take longer to complete. Use the **Fastest** option only for your final releases.

After you are done setting up the build settings (normally, the default settings work just fine), please make sure that you have added all your scenes to the build list, otherwise you will not be able to load that scene from the script. To add your current scene to the build list, go to **File | Build Settings** and click on the **Add Current** button. Once everything is good, click either the **Build** or **Build and Run** button. A window will pop out and ask you to key in the name of your game's executable. After that, click on **Save**.

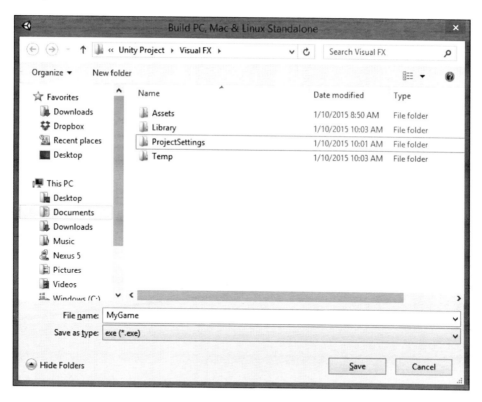

Then, Unity will start the process of building your game. It may take some time, depending on how many scenes you have and how many assets are linked to these scenes. The build process is quite different based on the target platform you've selected, and produces a different result too.

For web player, Unity will generate a .unity3d file that gets embedded into an HTML file. For PC, Unity will generate an executable and a data folder that keeps all the game assets in it. Mobile platforms such as iOS and Android are quite different; in this case, Unity will instead generate a project folder and launch its respective compiler (Xcode for iOS, Android SDK for Android) to build the game and deploy it directly to the mobile device. WebGL, on the other hand, is quite similar to the web player as it generates an HTML file too. However, instead of a .unity3d file, Unity will produce a bunch of JavaScript files that empower your game.

The entire build process is automated so you can sit down, drink a cup of coffee, and relax while waiting for it to finish the job!

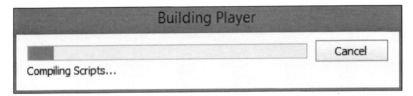

After your game has been built by Unity, you can then try to run your game! Since I'm building the game for PC, a graphics configuration window will pop out by default when the game is launched, which you can disable at the player settings; there will be more on that later. There are several options on the window, such as screen resolution, graphics quality, windowed mode, and monitor selection. You can also change the input mapping if you want to.

Click on **Play!** to start playing your game!

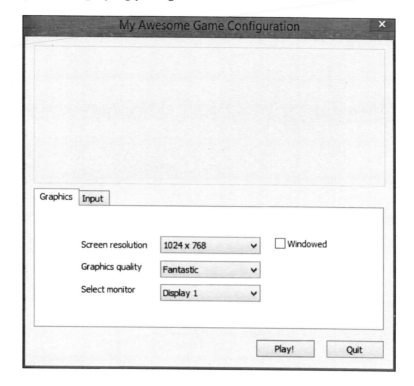

Player Settings

Even though you game has been successfully built and is now able to be playtested on the target platform, you may have already noticed that there are several things that look kind of odd. For instance, the game title has not been set, the game icon is showing the Unity logo, and several other things are not to your liking. Don't worry! This is because the player settings have not been properly configured.

To open up the player settings window, you can either go to **Edit** | **Project Settings** | **Player**, or go to **File** | **Build Settings** and click on the **Player Settings** button.

 Do note that the word **player** in this context does not mean the person who plays the game, but rather the system that runs the game and renders the graphics; in other words, the player application that is the build output.

You will see two different sections on the player settings window. The top section is the general settings of your game, such as your company name, product name, game icon, and so on. These settings are shared among the different platforms.

- **Company Name**: The name of your company. It will be used to locate the preferences file.

- **Product Name**: This will be displayed as the window title for the PC game or the display name below the icon for the mobile app. It will also be used to locate the preferences file.

- **Default Icon**: The default icon for your game on every platform. You can also override this for specific platforms.

- **Default Cursor**: The default cursor of your game. Only for platforms that support a cursor.

Cursor hotspot

Cursor hotspot in pixels from the top-left of the default cursor. You can set this to offset the hotspot position on your cursor used to simulate click.

At the bottom, you will see a long list of settings that are specific for the target platform you have selected. These settings are categorized into several different categories, such as **Resolution and Presentation, Icon, Splash Image**, and **Other Settings**. Each of these categories contains very different options depending on your target platform.

- **Resolution and Presentation**: This category contains all the settings related to your game's resolution, aspect ratio, screen orientation, and other options related to graphics rendering.

- **Icon**: You can override your game's icon for a specific platform by checking the **Override for [platform name]** option and selecting the icons you want underneath it.

- **Splash Image (Pro only)**: The splash image is the image shown while the game is launching. You can set your own splash image here if you're using Unity Pro.

- **Other Settings**: As the name implies, any other settings that do not fit in the preceding categories are placed within this category. It contains settings related to rendering, configuration, optimization, and so on, which again varies depending on the target platform.

- **Debugging and Crash Reporting (iOS only)**: This is an additional category for iOS related to debugging and crash reporting. You can set whether to log an uncaught exception in Objective-C, enable the CrashReport API, whether to silently exit or crash the game if there is an unhandled exception in .Net, and so on.

- **Publishing Settings (Android only)**: **Publishing Settings** is an additional category for Android that is used to set the keystore for your application before publishing it to the play store. You can also use the **Split Application Binary** option here.

Summary

Unity makes multiplatform publishing easy for game developers with just a click of a button, which traditionally costs a big sum of money just to port a game to a different platform. This has totally changed the landscape of game development, where smaller game developer teams are now able to publish their games for multiple platforms without worrying about the budget and technical know-how. On the other hand, big studios can also take advantage of this to reduce development risk and gain more sales to cover their enormous development costs.

We have now come to the end of the book. I hope you have gained the sufficient knowledge and acquired the skills to kickstart your first game project! I sincerely apologize if you think there is anything that I could have done better or if there is anything you feel is lacking in the book. Do contact me if there is. All the best!

Index

Thank you for buying
Building a Game with Unity and Blender

About Packt Publishing

Packt, pronounced 'packed', published its first book, *Mastering phpMyAdmin for Effective MySQL Management*, in April 2004, and subsequently continued to specialize in publishing highly focused books on specific technologies and solutions.

Our books and publications share the experiences of your fellow IT professionals in adapting and customizing today's systems, applications, and frameworks. Our solution-based books give you the knowledge and power to customize the software and technologies you're using to get the job done. Packt books are more specific and less general than the IT books you have seen in the past. Our unique business model allows us to bring you more focused information, giving you more of what you need to know, and less of what you don't.

Packt is a modern yet unique publishing company that focuses on producing quality, cutting-edge books for communities of developers, administrators, and newbies alike. For more information, please visit our website at www.packtpub.com.

About Packt Open Source

In 2010, Packt launched two new brands, Packt Open Source and Packt Enterprise, in order to continue its focus on specialization. This book is part of the Packt Open Source brand, home to books published on software built around open source licenses, and offering information to anybody from advanced developers to budding web designers. The Open Source brand also runs Packt's Open Source Royalty Scheme, by which Packt gives a royalty to each open source project about whose software a book is sold.

Writing for Packt

We welcome all inquiries from people who are interested in authoring. Book proposals should be sent to author@packtpub.com. If your book idea is still at an early stage and you would like to discuss it first before writing a formal book proposal, then please contact us; one of our commissioning editors will get in touch with you.

We're not just looking for published authors; if you have strong technical skills but no writing experience, our experienced editors can help you develop a writing career, or simply get some additional reward for your expertise.

Unity 3D Game Development by Example Beginner's Guide: LITE

ISBN: 978-1-84969-160-4   Paperback: 104 pages

Get up and running as a Unity game developer

1. Fast paced crash course in game design, programming, and Unity.

2. Build your first complete game in Unity.

3. Humorous writing style, serious content.

Blender 3D Basics
Beginner's Guide
Second Edition

ISBN: 978-1-78398-490-9   Paperback: 526 pages

A quick and easy-to-use guide to create 3D modeling and animation using Blender 2.7

1. Explore Blender's unique user interface and unlock Blender's powerful suite of modeling and animation tools.

2. Learn how to use Blender, and also the principles that make animation, lighting, and camera work come alive.

3. Start with the basics and build your skills through a coordinated series of projects to create a complex world.

Please check **www.PacktPub.com** for information on our titles

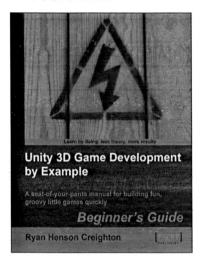

Unity 3D Game Development by Example Beginner's Guide

ISBN: 978-1-84969-054-6   Paperback: 384 pages

A seat-of-your-pants manual for building fun, groovy little games quickly

1. Build fun games using the free Unity 3D game engine even if you've never coded before.

2. Learn how to "skin" projects to make totally different games from the same file – more games, less effort!

3. Deploy your games to the Internet so that your friends and family can play them.

4. Packed with ideas, inspiration, and advice for your own game design and development.

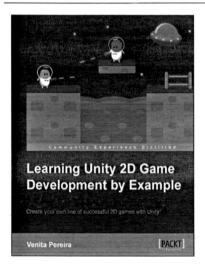

Learning Unity 2D Game Development by Example

ISBN: 978-1-78355-904-6   Paperback: 266 pages

Create your own line of successful 2D games with Unity!

1. Dive into 2D game development with no previous experience.

2. Learn how to use the new Unity 2D toolset.

3. Create and deploy your very own 2D game with confidence.

Please check **www.PacktPub.com** for information on our titles